Prometheus the Awakener

An Essay on
the Archetypal Meaning of
THE PLANET URANUS

Richard Tarnas

SPRING PUBLICATIONS
WOODSTOCK, CONNECTICUT

DUNQUIN SERIES 21

Published by Spring Publications, Inc.;
299 East Quassett Road;
Woodstock, Connecticut 06281.
Second printing 1998.
Manufactured in the province of Quebéc, Canada.
Text printed on acidfree paper.

Cover designed and produced by Margot McLean and SlobodanTrajkovic.
Cover image from the *Complete Encyclopedia of Illustration,*
by V. G. Heck (astronomy plates). Interior art: detail from Frontispiece
to the *Epitome of Ptolemy's Almagest,* by Johannes Müller
(Regiomontanus), Venice, 14596, reprinted from Charles Singer,
From Magic to Science (New York: Dover Publications, Inc., 1958).

Library of Congress Cataloging-in-Publication Data

Tarnas, Richard.
Prometheus the awakener : an essay on the
archetypal meaning of the planet Uranus / Richard Tarnas.
p.   cm. — (Dunquin series ; 21)
Includes bibliographical references.
ISBN 0-88214-21-6 (pbk.)
1. Astrology and psychology.   2. Archetype (Psychology)-
-Miscellanea.   3. Astrology and mythology.   4. Uranus (Planet)-
-Miscellanea.   5. Prometheus (Greek mythology)—Miscellanea.
I. Title.
BF17929.P8T37   1994
133.5'3—dc20   94-29645
                                                           CIP

To my son Christopher

Then felt I like some watcher of the skies
When a new planet swims into his ken . . .

John Keats
On First Looking into Chapman's Homer

CONTENTS

PREFACE

The initial insight that inspired this essay came to me suddenly in late 1978, in the week of the winter solstice, while I was living at Esalen Institute on the Pacific coast of Big Sur, California. For the previous several years, I had been working intensively with the meanings and manifestations of the planetary archetypes (and also spending long hours each night looking at the stars and planets in Big Sur's luminous night sky) when the new understanding of Uranus described in these pages opened up to me. I wrote the essay over the next few weeks and shared it privately with friends—Charles Harvey, Robert Hand, Stanislav Grof, and a few others—who I knew would be interested in the subject and could give me an informed response. I was delighted to find that, despite the radical nature of the thesis, these respected colleagues all embraced the identification as readily as had I.

In the following years, a number of journals requested permission to publish the essay—*National Council of Geocosmic Research Monographs* in 1981 (United States), *Spring 1983: An Annual of Archetypal*

Psychology and Jungian Thought (United States), *Journal of the Astrological Association* in 1989 (United Kingdom), *Journal of Astro Psychology* in 1990 (United States), *Galaxen* in 1992 (Denmark), and *Symbolon* in 1993 (Netherlands). Because of these several contexts, with differing requirements in terms of length and audience, over the years the essay ended up having multiple versions. The audience for the journal *Spring*, for example, was composed primarily of depth psychologists and scholars in the humanities rather than astrologers, and their professional interests affected the essay accordingly. In other cases, most of the astrological journals required the essay to be published in serial installments, and thus it had to be revised so as to be divisible into fairly self-sufficient, internally coherent parts.

In 1993, Auriel Press of Oxford, England, requested permission to publish the essay in more permanent form as a limited-edition small book, and so I took the opportunity to integrate these several parts and versions into its current form as a single integrated monograph. While doing so, I made a number of additions throughout the text, but in general Parts I–III derive from the version published in the *Journal of the Astrological Association*, while the long Part IV is adapted from the version published in *Spring 1983: An Annual of Archetypal Psychology and Jungian Thought*. Slight differences in style and approach will perhaps be noticed, but it was felt that these would be compensated for by the advantage of including in one publication a more extensive analysis of the topic than was previously available. I also added at this time an afterword, bringing the essay up to date with a discussion of the Uranus–Neptune cycle.

I am grateful to the many editors and readers who have expressed their appreciation for the essay over the years. And I am especially grateful to James Hillman, whose ideas and writings shaped the intellectual context in which I wrote the original essay fifteen years ago, and who has now honored it by bringing out this Spring Publications edition.

May 1994
San Francisco

I

URANUS AND PROMETHEUS

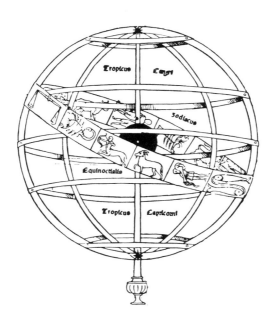

Planets and Archetypes

Awareness of an archetypal dimension of reality and its intimate participation in human affairs has over the centuries received perhaps its most sustained and precisely articulated expression in astrology. For at the heart of the astrological perspective is the recognition that the planets appear to possess a cosmically based connection to specific archetypal forces or principles which influence human existence, and that the planetary patterns in the heavens bear a meaningful relation to corresponding archetypal patterns in human affairs.

Archetypes can be understood and described in many ways, and indeed much of the history of Western thought from the ancient Greeks onward has revolved about this very issue. But for our present purposes, we may highlight three basic approaches toward this elusive yet crucial concept. The earliest form of the archetypal perspective, and in certain respects its deepest ground, is the primordial experience of the great gods and goddesses of ancient myth. In this mode of consciousness, memorably embodied at the dawn of Western culture in the Homeric epics, reality is understood to be pervaded and structured by powerful numinous forces and presences that are personified as mythic deities.

As the Greek mind evolved, in what is sometimes too simply described as a movement from myth to reason, these divine absolutes ordering the world were gradually deconstructed and then conceived anew in elaborate philosophic form in the dialogues of Plato. Building on the critical inquiries of his master Socrates, Plato gave to the archetypal perspective its classic metaphysical formulation. In the Platonic view, archetypes—the Ideas or Forms—are absolute essences that transcend the empirical world and yet give the world its form and meaning. They are timeless universals that serve as the fundamental reality informing any concrete particular (for example, something is beautiful to the exact extent that the archetype of Beauty is present in it). Direct knowledge of these Forms or Ideas is recognized as the spiritual goal of the philosopher and the intellectual passion of the scientist.[1]

Finally, the concept of archetypes unexpectedly reemerged in the twentieth century in the field of depth psychology when C. G. Jung, expanding on insights of Freud, described archetypes as autonomous primordial forms in the psyche that structure and impel human behavior and experience and that are expressions of a collective unconscious shared by all human beings. In the course of analyzing a vast range of psychological and cultural phenomena, Jung concluded that, although human experience was locally conditioned by a multitude of concrete biographical, cultural, and historical factors, subsuming all these at a deeper level appeared to be certain universal patterns or modes of experience, primordial forms that constantly arranged the elements of human experience into typical configurations and gave to collective human psychology a dynamic continuity. These archetypes endured as basic a priori symbolic forms while taking on the costume of the moment in each individual life and each cultural era, permeating each experience, each cognition, and each world view. In the words of James Hillman, archetypes "are cosmic perspectives in which the soul participates. They are the lords of its realms of being, the patterns for its mimesis. The soul cannot be, except in one of their patterns. All psychic reality is governed by one or another archetypal fantasy, given sanction by a God. I cannot but be in them."[2]

It is astrology's extraordinary insight that these complex, multidimensional archetypes which govern the forms of human experience are intelligibly connected with the planets and their movements in the heavens, an association that is observable in a constant coincidence between specific planetary alignments and specific corresponding archetypal phenomena in human affairs. In order to make sense of what follows, we need to understand the nature of this correspondence between planets and archetypes. It is not that astrologers have arbitrarily used the stories of the ancients about Venus, Mars, Mercury, and the rest to project symbolic meaning onto the planets, which are in actuality merely neutral material bodies without intrinsic significance. Rather, a considerable body of evidence suggests that the movements of the planets named Venus, Mars, and Mercury tend to coincide with patterns of human experience that closely resemble the character of their mythical counterparts. The astrologer's insight is fundamentally an empirical one. This empiricism is given context and meaning by a mythic, archetypal perspective, one that the planetary correlations seem to support and illustrate with remarkable consistency. The nature of these correlations presents to the astrological researcher what appears to be an orchestrated synthesis combining the precision of mathematical astronomy with the psychological profundity of poetic myth, a synthesis evidently existing a priori within the very fabric of the universe.

Here is where the distinction between the Jungian and the Platonic conceptions of archetypes becomes especially relevant, for while Jungian archetypes are considered to be the basic formal principles of the human psyche, Platonic archetypes are regarded as the essential principles of reality itself, rooted in the very nature of the cosmos. Mediating this debate between modern psychology and classical philosophy, astrology suggests that archetypes possess a reality that is both subjective and objective, informing both inner human psyche and outer cosmos. In effect, planetary archetypes are here recognized as being both Jungian and Platonic in nature—universal essences or forms at once intrinsic to and independent of the human mind—and are regarded as functioning in a Pythagorean-Platonic cosmic setting, i.e., in a cosmos that is pervasively integrated by virtue of some form of universal intelligence. From this perspective, what Jung called the collective unconscious can be viewed as being ultimately embedded within the cosmos itself, whose moving patterns are reflected in the dynamics of human experience. In Platonic terms, astrology suggests the existence of an *anima mundi* informing the cosmos, a world soul in which the human psyche participates.[3]

For conceptual clarity, then, a planetary archetype can be understood in three different senses: in the "Jungian" sense as a psychological principle, in the "Platonic" sense as a metaphysical essence, and in the "Homeric" sense as a mythological figure, all of these associated with a specific planet. Thus the archetype of Venus can be understood on the Homeric level as the Greek deity Aphrodite, the goddess of beauty and love, the Roman Venus. On the Platonic level, Venus can be understood in terms of the metaphysical principle of Eros and the Beautiful. And on the Jungian level, Venus can be understood as the psychological impulse and capacity to perceive, desire, create, or in some other way experience beauty and love, to attract and be attracted, to seek harmony and aesthetic or sensuous pleasure, to engage in artistic activity and in romantic and social relations. These different levels or senses, however, are distinguished here only to suggest the inherent complexity and ambiguity of archetypes, which must be formulated not as literal objects, but rather as autonomous patterns of meaning that cannot be localized or restricted to a specific dimension.

I have introduced these background considerations in order to call attention to an issue of some importance for modern astrology's theoretical foundations. It has long been an essential pillar of the astrological tradition that, when astrology was still united with astronomy, the ancients accurately named the visible planets—Sun, Moon, Mercury, Venus, Mars, Jupiter, Saturn—according to their actual archetypal nature, that is, according to their ruling mythic deity. All of the ancient planets were thus associated with archetypal principles having the essential character of their mythological namesakes, and modern astrological theory and practice has continued to endorse this basic correspondence.

Virtually all modern astrological researchers, on the basis of a large and continually growing body of data, believe that the ancient planets were correctly named; that is, the empirically evidenced astrological Mars corresponds in nature to the Mars of ancient mythology, the astrological Venus corresponds to the mythological Venus, the astrological Saturn to the mythological Saturn, and so forth. On the basis perhaps of a correct intuitive understanding, ancient astronomers assigned the names of the seven ancient planets, perceiving a cosmic conformity between the mythic deities and the visible planets.[4]

But the names of the three planets discovered by telescope in the modern era—Uranus, Neptune, and Pluto—were assigned by astronomers without any archetypal correspondences or considerations in mind. In turn, the astrological meanings of these planets were not based a priori upon their given names but were gradually determined by modern astrologers through observation and analysis. There is now virtually unanimous agreement among astrologers concerning those meanings. The question thus arises, what mythic archetypes actually underlie the observed astrological meanings for the three outer planets, and do these archetypes accurately correspond to those planets' given astronomical names? In the present essay I shall address this question with respect to the first of the modern planets, Uranus.

The New Planet

The seven planets known to the ancients formed what they believed was an absolute cosmic structure reflecting the primordial forces that governed human affairs. In 1781, however, an astronomer and musician named William Herschel, while conducting an exhaustive telescopic survey of the heavens, suddenly observed an object that was not an ordinary star. The object turned out to be the first planet to be discovered since prehistoric times. Herschel's stunning discovery immediately transformed the dimensions of the known solar system, the new planet being twice as far from the Sun as Saturn, but it also presented an unprecedented challenge to the astrological tradition. The ancient seven-planet hierarchy circumscribed by Saturn had been irrevocably disrupted, with no established archetypal meaning for the new planet.

Astronomers considered several names for the new planet. Herschel first proposed the name Georgium Sidus in honor of his sovereign patron, George III of England. The French, no doubt unenthusiastic about the planetary deification of an English monarch, used the name Herschel. But in the end, the pantheon of classical mythology was called upon; the German astronomer Johann Elert Bode had suggested the name Uranus in the year of its discovery, and this name eventually received international acceptance. The logic for naming the new planet Uranus seems to have been straightforward: the mythological Ouranos was the father of Saturn (Kronos), corresponding to the fact that the new planet was located beyond Saturn in the heavens— just as Saturn was the father of Jupiter in mythology and the next planet beyond Jupiter in the heavens. Ouranos was also the god of "the starry sky," as Hesiod called him, thus providing what seemed to be an especially apt name for the new planet.

Astrologers adopted the name Uranus as well, but the meaning they eventually attributed to the new planet was very different in character from that of the mythological Ouranos. The clear consensus among contemporary astrologers is that the planet Uranus is empirically associated with the principle of change, rebellion, freedom, liberation, reform and revolution, and the unexpected breakup of structures; with excitement, sudden surprises, lightning-like flashes of insight, revelations and awakenings; and with intellectual brilliance, invention, creativity, originality, and individualism. In addition to the occurrence of sudden breakthroughs and liberating events, Uranus transits are linked to unpredictable and disruptive changes, and thus the planet is often referred to as the "cosmic trickster." In terms of personal character, Uranus is regarded as signifying the individualist, the genius, and the rebel. These various qualities are considered to be so pronounced in persons born with a prominent Uranus, and expressed so conspicuously in a person's life during Uranus transits, that there seems to have been universal agreement among astrologers since at least the beginning of the twentieth century that these characteristics reflect the archetypal nature of the planet Uranus.

These observed qualities, however, bear little resemblance to the Greek mythic figure of Ouranos. Nothing in the mythological Ouranos's character suggests genius, rebellion, or the impulse for change. The tenor of the Ouranos myth is entirely different: he is the primordial god of the heavens, found in many mythologies, whose relationship to the Earth goddess Gaia forms part of the Greek creation myth. Indeed, Ouranos's role in that myth is not to initiate rebellion and change, but rather to resist it. The character of the mythological Ouranos not only diverges from but contradicts the meaning of the astrological Uranus. The mythological Ouranos encounters a revolt by his progeny and is overthrown; the astrological Uranus is regarded as quite the opposite—that which rebels and overthrows. None of the various qualities observed in connection with the planet Uranus—brilliance, freedom, unpredictability, invention, individualism, and so forth—has any plausible counterpart in the myth of Ouranos. Unlike the seven planets known to the ancients, the name of Uranus does not correspond with its astrological meaning. The name appears to have arisen from conventional eighteenth-century logic, not from archetypal insight.

I had been conscious of this discrepancy for some time when one day I noticed that those same astrological qualities fit another figure in Greek mythology with extraordinary precision. This figure was Prometheus, the Titan who rebelled against the gods, helped overthrow the tyrannical Kronos, tricked Zeus, and stole fire from Mount Olympus to liberate humanity from the gods' power. Prometheus was considered the wisest of his race and taught humankind all the arts and sciences. The more I examined the matter, the more I realized that every quality astrologers associate with the planet Uranus was reflected in the myth of Prometheus: the initiation of radical change, the passion for freedom, the defiance of authority, the act of cosmic rebellion against a universal structure to free humanity of bondage, the urge to transcend limitation, the intellectual brilliance and genius, the element of excitement and risk. So also Prometheus's style in outwitting the gods, when he used subtle stratagems and unexpected timing to upset the established order: he too was called the cosmic trickster. And the resonant symbol of Prometheus's fire conveyed at once several meanings—the creative spark, cultural and technological breakthrough, the enhancement of human autonomy, the liberating gift from the heavens, sudden enlightenment, intellectual and spiritual awakening—all of which astrologers consider to be connected with the planet Uranus.

I was unable to discover from the astrological literature exactly what basis had originally been used to determine Uranus's astrological meaning. It is possible that the unique (and, indeed, highly Promethean) character of the planet's discovery itself had suggested such a meaning—the sudden breakthrough from the heavens, the unexpected and unprecedented nature of the event, the crucial involvement of a technological invention (telescope), the disruption of tradition, the overthrow of past limits and structures. However, the earliest astrological texts I could find that discussed Uranus referred only to the character traits of persons with Uranus prominently placed at birth, implying that the study of natal charts had served as the principal basis for Uranus's definition.

More recent astrological sources suggested that the historical period of the planet's discovery in the late eighteenth century was relevant to its archetypal meaning—using the reasoning that the discovery of the physical planet in some sense represented an emergence of the planet's corresponding archetype into the conscious awareness of the collective psyche. In this regard the parallels with Uranus's astrological

14

meaning were certainly clear: the planet's discovery in 1781 occurred at the culmination of the Enlightenment, in the extraordinary era that brought forth the American and French Revolutions, the Industrial Revolution, and the age of Romanticism. In all these I could see as well the figure of Prometheus: the championing of human reason and individual autonomy; the challenge to traditional beliefs and customs; the revolt against royalty, aristocracy, established religion, social privilege, and political oppression; the Declarations of Independence and the Rights of Man, *liberté* and *egalité*; the beginnings of feminism; the widespread interest in radical ideas; the rapidity of change; the embrace of novelty; the celebration of human progress; the many inventions and technological advances; the revolutions in art and literature; the exaltation of the free human imagination and creative will; the plethora of geniuses and culture heroes. And here too were the Romantic poets with their great paeans to Prometheus himself. If the age of Uranus's discovery were to be given an archetypal characterization, none seemed more appropriate than "Prometheus Unbound."

Once I had noticed it, this correspondence between the astrological Uranus and the mythological Prometheus seemed to possess a certain intuitive self-evidence.[5] I could think of no quality, trait, or tendency observed in connection with the planet Uranus that was not captured in the myth and character of Prometheus. I thus began examining Uranus in natal charts, in transits, and in historical cycles, to see whether such an archetypal identification deepened my understanding of the relevant phenomena.

Sun–Uranus Natal Aspects

I first studied the possibility of a correlation between persons with significant Uranus aspects at birth and those whose life and character were notable for Promethean qualities, beginning with persons born with major aspects between Uranus and the Sun. Although of course all the planets are significant in natal chart analysis, I first looked at Sun aspects because of the Sun's basic association with the individual will and personal identity. If Prometheus was the actual archetypal figure corresponding to the planet Uranus, then one would expect persons born with the Sun in major aspect to Uranus to manifest certain Promethean qualities as central to their personality; and in the more outstanding cases, one might expect to find that the lives of such individuals would be especially notable for Promethean rebellion against traditional structures, for intellectual brilliance, originality, invention and innovation, radical change, individualistic self-expression, and so forth. With this thought in mind, I examined the

16

natal planetary positions for persons widely re-garded as major Promethean figures in Western cultural history.

What I shall present here is only a selection of the principal correlations that impressed me at the time and that led me on to other categories of evidence. Certainly no discussion of isolated configurations in a group of natal charts can do justice to the inherent complexity of those charts, which ultimately must be considered individually, each in its entirety and in relation to the full biography. But I was immediately struck by the nature of these initial correspondences suggesting the value of understanding the astrological Uranus in terms of the Prometheus archetype. For example, I first looked into the chief protagonists of the Scientific Revolution—Copernicus, Kepler, Galileo, Descartes, and Newton—since these men all appeared to be unambiguous representatives of the Prometheus archetype in both their intellectual character and their cultural role. Upon checking their planetary positions at birth, I found that every one of the five was born with Uranus in major aspect to the Sun well within conventional orbs (all natal aspects cited are listed with their degree of exactitude at the end of Part I). Similarly, when I then examined those who were the comparable founding revolutionaries of modern philosophy, I discovered that Descartes, Locke, and Kant were all born with this same configuration. So too was Freud, the founding revolutionary of modern psychology, and so also William James, one of the greatest pioneers in the history of psychology and the philosophical champion of human freedom in an open universe. All of these figures seemed to me especially apt embodiments of the Prometheus archetype, not only in the general sense of their all being intellectual revolutionaries and pioneers, but also in each one's particular role as a central protagonist in the larger Promethean project of advancing human autonomy.

I examined the natal planetary positions for many other similarly Promethean figures. For example, I checked at once the case of Percy Bysshe Shelley, since he was so explicitly associated—even identified—with Prometheus, his *Prometheus Unbound* being the pre-eminent work on that figure in modern literature. If the thesis that Uranus was actually Prometheus had any validity, the birth chart of Shelley would provide the most obvious test case. I found that in fact Shelley was born with the Sun and Uranus in close conjunction.

Moreover, both of his fellow Romantic poets Byron and Keats were born with the Sun and Uranus in major aspect as well (opposition and sextile). So too were other prominent Promethean cultural figures, such as Rousseau, the great catalyst of Romanticism in Europe, and Emerson, who played the same role in America. So also Jefferson, the pivotal figure in the American Revolution and in many ways an epitome of the Promethean Enlightenment. Or, more recently, Bob Dylan, the most influential figure in the countercultural revolution of the 1960s. When I looked for a comparable correspondence in the birth charts of women considered Promethean by virtue of their independence of spirit, creative originality, or rebellion against traditional structures, I was similarly impressed; thus, for example, Marie Curie, Margaret Mead, Gertrude Stein, Mary Shelley, Madame de Staël, George Sand, Susan B. Anthony, Beatrice Webb, and Simone de Beauvoir were all born with the Sun and Uranus in major aspect.[6]

Of course, innumerable other men and women were born with Sun–Uranus aspects who were not Shelleys or Galileos or Marie Curies. In considering the various persons of my acquaintance who had such a natal aspect but were not prominent cultural figures, I noticed that in these cases the Prometheus archetype was indeed still visible in their lives and characters, expressed less spectacularly than in the well-known cases, yet nevertheless in ways that distinctly reflected the basic archetype: i.e., persons who were inventive or innovative in small ways, or who were markedly out of the ordinary in some sense but not famously so, erratic and unpredictable persons, individuals who more than most sought their own paths in life, people with rebellious or eccentric temperaments who were otherwise unexceptional, those persons drawn to unusual or exciting experiences, those attracted to novel or radical ideas, and so forth.

That a given natal aspect can express itself in a virtually limitless variety of ways and yet consistently reflect the underlying nature of the relevant archetypes is of course not only characteristic of all astrological correspondence but essential to it. Astrology is not concretely predictive. It is archetypally predictive. A major aspect between two planets indicates a mutual activation of the corresponding archetypes, but the specific character of the final result is not predetermined by the existence of that aspect. Two different persons could be born with the same two planets in the same close major aspect, but for one person the power and quality of the archetypal stimulus might be considerably greater than for the other, and that difference might not necessarily be discernible in the natal chart. Or the archetype might express itself in one way rather than another (for instance, as juvenile delinquency rather than scientific innovation), both ways being equally appropriate to the specific archetype in question. From this perspective, the investigation of major cultural figures is valuable not because they alone were born with the aspects in question, which they were not, but rather because their lives and characters expressed specific archetypal traits in an especially conspicuous and publicly assessable manner.

Moon–Uranus Natal Aspects

As I moved on to the examination of natal Uranus aspects involving planets other than the Sun, distinct archetypal differentiations emerged that corresponded closely to the nature of the other planets involved. For example, given the Moon's association with the archetypal feminine principle, I was curious what I would find in the case of men who had major Moon–Uranus aspects at birth.

Here I found a comparison of Freud's and Jung's birth charts instructive, for while Freud was born with Uranus in conjunction to the Sun, Jung's most prominent Uranus aspect was a close square to the Moon. In light of the archetypal polarity between the Sun and Moon, I thought it interesting that while Freud focused his therapeutic work on the masculine Oedipus archetype, whose working through he saw as necessary for freeing the psyche from infantile dependence and fixations, Jung focused on the feminine anima archetype, whose integration he saw as necessary for the psyche's liberation from unconsciousness and imbalance.

And in general, Jung's psychology, his imagery

and mythology, was far more "feminine" in archetypal character—animistic, receptive and reflective, intuitive, artistic, concerned with mystery and ambiguity and soul—while Freud's was more archetypally "masculine"—realist, active and interventionist, rational, scientific. Freud's concern was with the ego and its heroic struggle against the id, with confronting the instinctual unconscious and exposing it to the clear rational light of day. Jung, on the other hand, called attention to the spontaneously creative and integrative qualities of the unconscious, personified as the anima, and was more likely to describe the psyche in terms that stressed its irreducible depths and all-encompassing nature. While Freud's ideas favored masculine concerns and patriarchal assumptions, Jung argued specifically for the elevation of the feminine to a position of balance in the cultural psyche. Whereas Freud wrote at length about the Primal Father, Jung repeatedly addressed the Great Mother. Freud's religious concern was almost exclusively with paternal monotheism, while Jung often treated the polytheistic and matriarchal. In later life Freud wrote on Moses, Jung on Mary and Sophia. From the beginning Freud's closest and most brilliant students were typically men; Jung's were women. As an overall pattern, Freud's Promethean impulse seemed to be associated both personally and theoretically more with the masculine principle while Jung's was linked more to the feminine.[7]

This same association between the feminine and the Promethean in a man born with the Moon and Uranus in aspect I also noted in the case of George Bernard Shaw, born with a conjunction between the two planets. Here I was struck by the fact that, although Shaw advocated many forms of radical and revolutionary ideas throughout his life, he appears to have especially identified his own freedom with that of women. He was an early and vigorous supporter of women's liberation and their rebellion against oppressive social structures. In his plays, the most vibrant portraits were those of independent, free-minded women—the heroines of *Pygmalion, Major Barbara, Mrs. Warren's Profession, Arms and the Man, Candida*, even *Man and Superman*. When treating the theme of religious rebel as saint, he chose a woman, Joan of Arc, in *Saint Joan*. He wrote the encyclopedic political tract *The Intelligent Woman's Guide to Socialism and Capitalism*. Many of his most important friendships were with women, themselves notably Promethean in character—Ellen Terry, Mrs. Patrick Campbell, Annie Besant. In Shaw's case as in Jung's, the association of the Prometheus archetype with the feminine again seemed to correspond with a natal Uranus–Moon aspect.

Similarly, among contemporary women, I

found that both of the feminist leaders Betty Friedan and Germaine Greer were born with the Moon and Uranus in major aspect. In these women the Promethean impulse of change and liberation was specifically linked to issues of female identity, marriage, motherhood, the bearing and raising of children, family and domestic life, the role of the wife, emotional and psychological factors in women's lives, relations with other women, the female body, as well as the nature of the feminine principle in general—all basic themes of the Moon archetype.[8]

Uranus–Pluto and the Sixties

Correlations such as these suggested to me the value of interpreting the planet Uranus in terms of the archetype of Prometheus, and I shall discuss further archetypal patterns involving Prometheus in personal biographies when I examine other natal Uranus configurations in a later part of this essay. It was, however, in the study of the larger historical planetary cycles that I found the Uranus–Prometheus correspondence especially useful. To mention but one example here, I noticed at once that the great Uranus–Pluto conjunction of the 1960s could be superbly understood as a profound manifestation of the Prometheus archetype being empowered and compelled by Pluto on a massive scale across the world: thus the tremendous wave of revolutionary protest movements that dominated the period, the civil rights movement, the antiwar movement, the acceleration of independence movements throughout the Third World, the pervasive influence of radical political philosophies, the crescendo of student activism and the multitude of marches, strikes, and demonstrations from Berkeley and Washington to Paris and Tokyo. Here too emerged the feminist movement, the ecology movement, the human potential movement, the widespread challenge to established beliefs and the embrace of radically new intellectual perspectives, the broad rebirth of interest in esoteric disciplines such as astrology, the profound revolutions in theology and the Christian churches, the restless drive toward innovation and experiment that affected virtually all the arts, the spectacular musical creativity of the decade, the extraordinary eruption and flourishing of the American and European youth counterculture, the pervasive spirit of rebellion against "the Establishment" in all its forms, the radical questioning of all conventions and traditions.

Moreover, the empowerment of the Prometheus archetype was equally visible during the 1960s in terms of that decade's unprecedented scientific and technological advances in so many areas, most dramatically in the epochal achievements in space exploration and the landing of astronauts on the moon. And so also was the era marked by another important characteristic of the Prometheus archetype—the powerful sense of intellectual and spiritual awakening which was felt by so many at the time. Uranus and Pluto were conjunct only once this century, and the decade in which this occurred, the 1960s, was the most conspicuously and potently Promethean of the century. I believe no other archetype better expresses and comprehends the character of that era, with its impassioned demand for freedom and titanic quest for new horizons.[9]

Natal Uranus Aspects Cited in Text

Nicolaus Copernicus	4°22'	Uranus trine Sun
Johannes Kepler	6°47'	Uranus conjunct Sun
Galileo Galilei	1°46'	Uranus square Sun
Rene Descartes	5°28'†	Uranus conjunct Sun
Isaac Newton	1°34'†	Uranus sextile Sun
John Locke	8°36'†	Uranus conjunct Sun
Immanuel Kant	0°08'	Uranus opposite Sun
Sigmund Freud	4°16'	Uranus conjunct Sun
William James	0°02'†	Uranus sextile Sun
Percy Bysshe Shelley	5°52'	Uranus conjunct Sun
Lord Byron	4°20'	Uranus opposite Sun
John Keats	0°54'†	Uranus sextile Sun
Jean-Jacques Rousseau	2°50'†	Uranus sextile Sun
Ralph Waldo Emerson	3°56'	Uranus trine Sun
Thomas Jefferson	3°38'†	Uranus square Sun
Bob Dylan	6°53'	Uranus conjunct Sun

URANUS AND PROMETHEUS

Marie Curie	1°52'†	Uranus trine Sun
Margaret Mead	6°26'	Uranus conjunct Sun
Gertrude Stein	6°21'	Uranus opposite Sun
Mary Shelley	4°52'	Uranus conjunct Sun
Madame de Staël	6°42'†	Uranus conjunct Sun
George Sand	2°49'†	Uranus square Sun
Susan B. Anthony	1°54'†	Uranus sextile Sun
Beatrice Webb	6°59'†	Uranus trine Sun
Simone de Beauvoir	4°25'	Uranus conjunct Sun
C. G. Jung	1°17'	Uranus square Moon
George Bernard Shaw	2°57'	Uranus conjunct Moon
Betty Friedan	1°19'	Uranus sextile Moon
Germaine Greer	3°19'	Uranus conjunct Moon
Wolfgang Amadeus Mozart	4°36'	Uranus square Moon
Orson Welles	3°13'	Uranus conjunct Moon
Jackie Coogan	0°39'	Uranus conjunct Moon
Shirley Temple	5°49'	Uranus square Moon
Lord Byron	2°52'	Uranus conjunct Moon
Oscar Wilde	0°30'	Uranus square Moon

† ± < 0°32' (date only, calc. for noon).

II

THE URANUS TRANSIT CYCLE

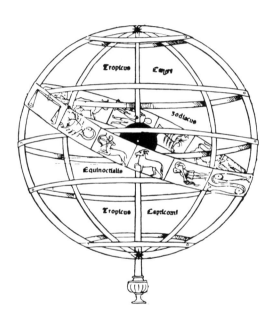

In Part I of this essay I discussed the discrepancy between the planet Uranus's name and its archetypal significance and pointed out that, while the astrological Uranus bore little resemblance to the mythological Ouranos, it corresponded with remarkable precision to the mythological Prometheus. I then cited a number of examples of outstanding Promethean individuals who had Uranus prominent in their natal charts, in order to suggest the increased conceptual clarity and depth of insight I found by interpreting the planet Uranus in terms of the archetype of Prometheus. In this section I shall cite another category of evidence, involving the Uranus transit cycle, which I found equally illuminating.

Because transits tend to coincide so consistently with events and experiences whose character closely corresponds to the relevant planetary archetypes—"activating the potential" of the natal chart—I was interested in discovering whether transits involving the planet Uranus tended to coincide with events and experiences of a distinctly Promethean character. In particular I wanted to investigate whether the Prometheus archetype would be especially visible when Uranus was involved on both sides of the transit—that is, when Uranus was both the transiting planet currently in the sky and the natal planet being transited. It takes Uranus approximately eighty-four years to complete a full 360° sidereal cycle and return in conjunction to its original position at a person's birth. Thus of the two climactic points of the Uranus transit cycle, the conjunction and opposition, the former would occur only when and if a person reached approximately eighty-four years of age. In looking for possible correlations in the Uranus cycle, I therefore decided first to examine the Uranus opposition transit, with Uranus at the 180° point of its cycle, for the occurrence of events having a specifically Promethean character.

The first case I examined was that of Sigmund Freud, and it was here I first perceived the pattern I would subsequently find with such frequency. In Freud's life, transiting Uranus was in the opposition phase of its cycle, within 5° of exact 180° alignment from its position at Freud's birth, during the period from November 1894 to September 1897. I recalled these years as being of pivotal importance in Freud's life and in the emergence of psychoanalysis, but to verify exact dates and events I consulted the standard biography by Ernest Jones.[1] I found that in the spring of 1895, Freud and his colleague Josef Breuer published *Studies on Hysteria*, with whose final chapter on psychotherapy by Freud "it is customary to date the beginnings of psychoanalysis."[2] On 24 July 1895, Freud first fully analyzed one of his dreams, the "dream of Irma's injection." Called by Jones a "historic occasion," this date was referred to by Freud as that on which "the secret of dreams was revealed" to him.[3] Freud later wrote, "Insight such as this falls to one's lot but once in a lifetime."[4] Breuer wrote in the summer of 1895 that "Freud's intellect is soaring at its highest. I gaze after him as a hen at a hawk."[5] During these years Freud postulated the latent wish-fulfillment function of dreams, formulated the distinction between primary and secondary mental processes, and developed his views on the sexual etiology of neurosis, the existence of infantile eroticism, and the nature of the conscious ego with its resistance to the instincts. This period also brought the first mention of the fundamental concepts of compromise formation, over-determination, the return of the repressed, and erotogenic zones. At this time, wrote Jones, "Freud was in his most revolutionary stage, both intellectually and emotionally."[6]

Other major events occurred during this period. The term "psychoanalysis" was first used in a paper completed on 5 February 1896. During the same year, Freud renounced hypnosis as a therapeutic measure in favor of free association, thereafter the standard method for psychoanalysis. *The*

Interpretation of Dreams, the foundational work of psychoanalysis on which he would labor for the rest of the decade, was according to Freud "finished in all essentials at the beginning of 1896."[7] In the spring of 1897 Freud first began developing his conception of the Oedipal conflict. And in the summer of 1897 Freud commenced his systematic self-analysis, generally considered the most important turning point of Freud's intellectual and psychological evolution.

This wave of events that coincided with Freud's Uranus-opposite-Uranus transit seemed to reflect a distinct climax in the unfolding of Freud's Promethean impulse, giving the impression that the opposition represented a "Full Moon" moment for the Prometheus archetype in the lifelong Uranus cycle. The correlations were sufficiently striking that I began to investigate cases of other major scientific revolutionaries, in each instance comparing the astronomical situation with the biographical data. In the case of Galileo, perhaps the classic Promethean figure in the history of science, I found that Uranus had reached the opposition point of its cycle within 5° orb during the period from July 1607 to June 1610. It was in the fall of 1609 that Galileo had first turned the telescope to the heavens, there discovering the craters on the Moon, the moons of Jupiter, the numerous individual stars of the Milky Way, and other celestial phenomena supportive of the Copernican hypothesis, and it was on 12 March 1610 that he published *Sidereus Nuncius* (The Starry Messenger), the epoch-making account of his observations. During these several months Uranus was within 3° of exact opposition to its placement at Galileo's birth, and on the day of the book's publication Uranus was within 1°. Again it seemed that, in the life of a pathbreaking individual, the midpoint of the Uranus cycle represented an unmistakably climactic moment in the unfolding of that person's Promethean impulse.

I then examined the life of Newton and found that Uranus was at the opposition point of its cycle from May 1686 to April 1689. Newton published his *Principia*, the foundational work of modern science in which he formulated the three laws of motion and the law of universal gravitation, on 5 July 1687. On that day Uranus was 1° from exact opposition to its placement at Newton's birth.

In the case of Descartes, I found that Uranus reached the opposition point of its cycle during the period from October 1635 to August 1638. On 8 June 1637, Descartes published his most significant work, the *Discourse on Method*, the foundational work of modern philosophy in which Descartes set forth his basic philosophical doctrines, including his rationalist methodology and the *cogito* argument. He also published in that period his *Geometry*, the founding work of modern analytic geometry which first introduced the Cartesian coordinates and the use of algebra for solving geometrical problems. Again, at the time these works were published, Uranus was within 1° of exact opposition to its location at Descartes's birth.

When I checked the case of Francis Bacon, I found that Uranus reached the opposition point of its cycle during the period from June 1604 to May 1607. In October 1605, Bacon published *The Advancement of Learning*, his foundational philosophical treatise setting forth his vision of scientific knowledge as the key to human progress. And again at that time Uranus was within 1° of exact opposition to its location at Bacon's birth.

A more complex pattern emerged in the case of Albert Einstein. In this instance, Uranus had reached the 180° opposition point of its cycle during the years 1918–1921. In November 1919, the Royal Society in London announced that its scientific expedition to Principe Island, formed for the purpose of photographing a solar eclipse earlier that year, had completed calculations demonstrating a deflection of light at the rim of the Sun, thereby giving dramatic support to Einstein's general theory of relativity. Einstein was immediately heralded as a genius without precedent, and the theory of relativity was for the first time widely acclaimed by both the scientific community and the larger public.

Yet this was only one of two great turning points

in Einstein's life. The first, and in terms of Einstein's own scientific development the more critically important one, had occurred in the summer and fall of 1905, when he had published four papers in the scientific journal *Annalen der Physik*. These papers, which were to transform modern physics, presented the special theory of relativity, the equivalence of mass and energy, the theory of Brownian motion, and the photon theory of light. When I checked the position of Uranus at that time, I found that Uranus was at the 120° trine point of its cycle during the years 1904–06. On the day that *Annalen der Physik* received Einstein's epoch-making paper on special relativity—30 June 1905—Uranus was within 1° of exact aspect to its position at Einstein's birth.

Precisely this latter correlation occurred also in the case of Charles Darwin. Uranus had reached the 180° opposition point of its cycle in Darwin's life during the years 1852–55. These were productive and not unimportant years for Darwin's scientific work, when he was deeply involved in research concerning the variation and classification of species, yet the period did not seem genuinely comparable to the previous correspondences I had come upon. However, I then checked earlier in Darwin's life to see when Uranus had reached the 120° trine point of its cycle. I found that this had occurred in the period from February 1837 through December 1839, which was indeed when Darwin first formu-

lated the theory of evolution in his private note-
books. In 1837, soon after his return from the *Beagle*
expedition to South America and the Galapagos
Islands, Darwin had recognized that many of his
observations could only be understood if species
changed over time and evolved in different direc-
tions from a common ancestor. But the theory
lacked a mechanism by which evolution took place
until, on 28 September 1838, Darwin read Malthus's
Essay on the Principle of Population with its theory of
the necessary relation of human population growth
to food supply. Extrapolating from Malthus's idea,
Darwin realized that nature enforced its selection
of species by eliminating those variations that could
not fit into available ecological niches and favoring
those that could. On that day, Darwin entered into
his "Notebook on the Transmutation of Species" the
note that demonstrated he had solved the problem
of natural selection. Also on that day, transiting Uranus was within 1° of exact aspect to its position at
Darwin's birth.

As I continued examining cases of this sort, the
nature of the evidence seemed to favor the existence
of a genuine correlation between the Uranus transit cycle and activations of the Prometheus archetype, visible in the specific timing of these various
events and breakthroughs. Of course other factors
were relevant for assessing the character and timing
of these correlations, such as the specific planets

aspecting Uranus in the natal chart, other concurrent transits, the presence of midpoint configurations, and so forth. And many comparable events of Promethean character coincided with transits in which either Uranus was transiting another important point in the natal chart (e.g., Uranus transiting natal Sun) or another outer planet was transiting natal Uranus (e.g., Pluto transiting natal Uranus). Yet the Uranus cycle on its own terms appeared to represent an especially significant cyclical pattern for the unfolding Prometheus impulse.

For example, I found that the first two quadrature points of the Uranus cycle, the square and opposition, precisely coincided with the two famous periods of Newton's life that brought forth his most important achievements. In his early twenties, during the years 1664–66, Newton laid most of the foundations for his later work—developing the binomial theorem and the calculus, performing advanced research in optics, and deriving the inverse square relation for planetary motion; this was also when the incident of the falling apple occurred. "In two short years, summer 1664 to October 1666, Newton the mathematician was born, and in a sense the rest of his creative life was largely the working out, in calculus as in his mathematical thought in general, of the mass of burgeoning ideas which sprouted in his mind on the threshold of intellectual maturity."[8] Newton himself wrote of this period, "I was in the prime of my age for invention and minded Mathematics and Philosophy more than at any time since."[9]

During just these years, from January 1664 to December 1666, Uranus was at the 90° point of its cycle, 5° orb. Thus a perfect symmetrical pattern was visible: these early discoveries, which were the necessary forerunners of the *Principia*, occurred when Uranus had moved 90° from its position at Newton's birth, while the *Principia* itself was written when Uranus had moved exactly 90° further, to form the 180° opposition.

This instance of a major intellectual breakthrough occurring in coincidence with the first Uranus-square-Uranus transit, which takes place in a person's late teens and early twenties, was relatively rare, certainly on anything near the level of Newton's achievement. Einstein's and Darwin's breakthroughs, for example, occurred during the next major aspect of the Uranus cycle, the trine. Yet of course the Uranus-square-Uranus transit is regularly found to coincide with another, equally vivid manifestation of the Prometheus archetype, that of youthful rebellion, as this is typically the period when youth makes its first fundamental break from structures established or upheld by the previous generation. Similarly with the opposition, the second quadrature aspect of the Uranus cycle: occurring in one's late thirties and early forties, the Uranus-opposite-

Uranus transit tends to coincide with the midlife crisis (often called a "second adolescence"), again a period of unmistakably Promethean character, in which men and women often feel driven to break out of conventional structures—social, professional, psychological—to seek greater freedom, creative self-expression, and so forth.

An instructive case in this latter category, and indeed a paradigmatic example of the Prometheus impulse acting in a woman's life, is that of Betty Friedan. Uranus transited in opposition to Friedan's natal Uranus in 1962–63, and it was precisely during these years that she wrote and published her landmark feminist work *The Feminine Mystique*. With its influential criticism of the traditional restriction of women to domestic and child-rearing roles, the book inspired a generation of women to discard inherited patriarchal assumptions and to press for equal role-sharing between the sexes.

Paradigmatic cases are always of great relevance in astrological research, and thus I was naturally interested in the transits for Friedrich Nietzsche's *Thus Spoke Zarathustra*, perhaps the most profound and certainly the most titanic work of the Prometheus impulse in philosophy and world literature. Nietzsche was born with Uranus in conjunction with Jupiter; precisely during the period 1883–85 in which Uranus transited in opposition to this natal complex (conjoining natal Mars and Mercury), in a great creative explosion Nietzsche brought forth *Zarathustra*—completing the final part in early 1885 just as Uranus moved within 1° of exact opposition to its location at Nietzsche's birth.

Similarly in the case of Dostoevsky's *Crime and Punishment*: Uranus was at the opposition point of its cycle from June 1864 to May 1867, which exactly coincided with the period in which Dostoevsky wrote this, the first of his great novels, begun in 1865 and completed in 1866. Though he had written a number of works prior to this, Dostoevsky's creativity was at its height beginning with the time of the Uranus opposition.

Another exemplary case was that of Oscar Wilde. Although he wrote much of value in the course of his life, he composed one undisputed masterpiece, *The Importance of Being Earnest*, the greatest farce in the language. This play was written during the two months of August and September 1894. Uranus was at the opposition point of its cycle in Wilde's life from January 1893 to November 1895.

An especially appropriate test-case of the Uranus cycle's relation to the Prometheus archetype was that of Shelley and the writing of *Prometheus Unbound*. Shelley died young, having drowned at sea off the coast of Italy when he was twenty-nine (during his Saturn return), and thus Uranus never reached the 180° opposition point of its cycle during the poet's lifetime. Looking back, however, I found that Uranus had reached the 120° trine during the period from January 1817 to December 1819. Shelley wrote *Prometheus Unbound* in 1818–19, completing the last act in December 1819.

These various instances in which Promethean works had been produced in the first half of life prodded me into checking the case of Immanuel Kant, who, unlike most of the persons I had examined, was notable for how late in life he had produced his principal work, *The Critique of Pure Reason*. The latter was published in 1781, long after Uranus had reached both the 120° and 180° points in its cycle. When I checked Uranus's position in that year, I found it had exactly reached the second trine: 240° from its position at Kant's birth, 120° away from reaching conjunction at the end of its cycle. I found of equal interest the fact that, earlier in Kant's life, transiting Uranus had been in the opposition point of its cycle during the years 1766–69, which was the period in which Kant first conceived the germinal idea that formed the basis for *The Critique of Pure Reason*—the "critical" epistemological insight which revolutionized modern philosophy.

So too with John Locke, who did not publish his major works until his later years—*An Essay Concerning Human Understanding* and *Two Treatises of Government*, both in 1690, and *A Letter Concerning Toleration* in 1689. Transiting Uranus was at the second trine position of its cycle in Locke's life during the years 1688–91. And, as with Kant, the earlier period of the Uranus opposition transit had coincided with the pivotal early development of Locke's major philosophical ideas in the 1670s.

With these cases before me, I began to find similar patterns in other persons whose creative work extended well into the second half of life. For example, Cervantes published his magnum opus, *Don Quixote*, in January 1605, which was exactly when Uranus had reached the second trine point of its cycle. Similarly, although Dostoevsky wrote his first masterpiece, *Crime and Punishment*, in 1865–66 when Uranus was at the opposition point of its cycle, he wrote his culminating work, *The Brothers Karamazov*, in 1878–80 when Uranus had reached the second trine just before his death. So also Bacon, having published his first major work in the philosophy of science, *The Advancement of Learning*, in 1605 when Uranus was at the opposition point of its cycle, went on to publish his culminating work, *Novum Organum*, in 1620 when Uranus had reached the second trine.[10]

Many of these correlations suggested the possibility that there existed within each life a significant connection and continuity between events that coincided with the successive major alignments of the Uranus transit cycle. I was therefore curious whether there were in any of these cases an example of someone living long enough for Uranus to complete its full 360° cycle, thereby reaching con-junction with its original position at the person's birth. Recalling that Freud had lived to his eighty-fourth year, I discovered that just as Uranus was reaching the point of conjunction in the summer of 1938, when Freud was compelled by the Nazis' presence in Vienna to move to London for the last months of his life, he had written his succinctly definitive summary of psychoanalytic theory, *An Out-line of Psychoanalysis*. His last book, the celebrated *Outline* was in effect a synopsis of his life's work. This same period also saw the completion and publica-tion of Freud's *Moses and Monotheism*, the book that had long occupied his attention and that analyzed the Promethean figure with whom Freud had had a lifelong identification.

This in turn impelled me to examine the case of the similarly long-lived Jung. When the Uranus cycle in his life reached completion, with Uranus moving across the point of conjunction from Sep-tember 1957 to July 1960, Jung composed his own celebrated summing up, *Memories, Dreams, Reflections.* Thus both Freud and Jung had written retrospec-tive summaries of their life's work precisely during the period coincident with Uranus's conjunction to itself at the end of its cycle.

In Freud's case I now noticed a striking pattern: the 180° halfway point of the Uranus cycle which occurred in the 1890s had coincided with his period of major breakthrough—the beginning of his self-analysis, his formulation of the basic concepts of psychoanalysis, and the start of writing his foundational work, *The Interpretation of Dreams*—while the 360° point of the cycle's completion coincided with his lifework summations, the *Outline of Psychoanalysis* and *Moses and Monotheism*. Looking back to Jung's earlier life, I found that the 180° point of his Uranus cycle had occurred during the period from early 1914 to early 1917: these were in fact the years of his most intensive and systematic self-analysis, a period of psychological crisis and breakthrough precisely parallel to that of Freud, out of which Jung emerged with his fundamental concepts concerning the archetypes of the collective unconscious, the anima and the Self, the transcendent function, the process of individuation, and the internal objectivity of psychic reality. Later, in *Memories, Dreams, Reflections*, Jung spoke of this time as the most important in his life, the source of virtually all his subsequent scientific and psychological insights.[11] Just as with Freud, this pivotal period coincided with the halfway point of Jung's Uranus cycle, while the cycle's completion coincided with his retrospective life summary. The symmetry of these patterns seemed to me remarkable.

Finally, a very recent example of this same pattern (though with an interesting difference) is the case of the great mythologist Joseph Campbell.

Campbell's pivotal work and the one with which he will always be most closely identified—*The Hero with a Thousand Faces*, a work conspicuously Promethean in both its subject and its character—was published in 1949. At this time Uranus was precisely at the 180° point in its cycle. Campbell lived to be 83, dying in October 1987 just before Uranus reached the completion of its 360° cycle. Then, during the year following his death and in exact coincidence with the Uranus return transit, his work suddenly achieved unprecedented public attention as a result of the posthumous television broadcasts of the Moyers interviews and a wave of published and filmed works devoted to Campbell's life and ideas.

The occurrence of such posthumous correlations was in fact noted by Jung himself. In a valuable lecture on Jung's birth chart delivered in 1974 in Zürich, his daughter Gret Baumann-Jung mentioned the following anecdote: "Shortly before his death, as we talked about horoscopes, my father remarked: 'The funny thing is that the darned stuff even works after death.' "[12]

III

URANUS ASPECTS
WITH INNER PLANETS

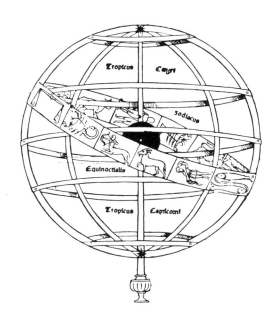

In the first two parts of this essay, I set forth a number of reasons for considering that the archetypal figure corresponding to the planet Uranus was not in fact the Ouranos of Greek myth, the somewhat oppressive ruler of the sky and husband of Gaia, but was rather Prometheus, the pre-eminent mythic personification of rebellion, revolution, technological and cultural innovation, and the striving for freedom and change. In Part II, I examined a series of extraordinary scientific and intellectual breakthroughs—Freud's first major psychoanalytic discoveries, Galileo's first turning his telescope to the heavens, Newton's writing of the *Principia*, Darwin's discovery of the theory of evolution, Einstein's writing his paper on the special theory of relativity, and several others—all of which were unambiguously Promethean in character and all of which happened to coincide with major alignments of the individual's Uranus transit cycle. Earlier, in Part I, I described how I had initially pursued this correspondence between the planet Uranus and the archetype of Prometheus by examining the natal charts of major cultural figures whose personal lives and cultural influence were widely regarded as Promethean in character. While my focus there was on Uranus natal aspects to the Sun or Moon, we now turn our attention to another set of correlations—Uranus in aspect to Mars, Venus, or Mercury—which suggest some further ways in which the individual expression of the Prometheus archetype appears to be inflected according to which planet is in aspect to Uranus.

Again, no analysis of isolated configurations in a group of natal charts can ever do justice to the intrinsic complexity of those charts. For the sake of clarity and simplicity I have restricted the present discussion to major natal aspects involving Uranus, without distinguishing between the different aspects involved (conjunction, square, etc.) and without attending to the many other factors relevant to natal chart analysis. Certainly in the long run, every example cited would be more properly studied in the context of the full natal chart with all its planetary aspects, midpoint configurations, and so forth, whose examination would render a considerably more complicated and nuanced view of things than the present discussion can suggest. But such is the inevitable price of all analysis, by which wholes are broken down conceptually into parts in order to mediate a provisionally better understanding.

I had already noted an interesting differentiation in the expression of the Prometheus archetype when I had compared Moon–Uranus natal aspects with Sun–Uranus ones, observing for example how the characteristic association of the Promethean with the feminine in Jung's life and ideas coincided with his natal Moon–Uranus aspect, while Freud's equally decisive association of the Promethean with the masculine had coincided with a Sun–Uranus aspect. Turning now to aspects between Uranus and Mars, and considering what would be the logical result of combining Prometheus with the archetype of the warrior, my first thought was of Napoleon, in whose life both brilliant military ability and the spread of the French Revolution were central elements. I found that Napoleon was in fact born with Uranus and Mars in close major aspect, a trine (all natal aspects cited are listed with their degree of exactitude at the end of this section). Similarly, I found that both Lenin and Mao—the two men who had led the most important political revolutions of the twentieth century, both of them also pre-eminent theorists of violent revolution—were born with Mars and Uranus in major aspect as well. I was also interested to find that Nietzsche, the philosopher most notable for the militancy and aggressiveness of his intellectual rebellion, was born with Mars and Uranus in close major aspect (Uranus opposite his Mercury–Mars conjunction). In these and similar instances the presence of a Mars–Uranus aspect appeared to signify an emphatic joining together of the Mars impulse of assertiveness, aggression, and militancy with the Promethean tendency toward radical change, revolution, and liberation.

The combination of Uranus with Venus was equally suggestive. Considering Venus's association with beauty and art, I checked the case of Leonardo da Vinci and found that he was indeed born with Venus and Uranus in close major aspect. Again, just as Napoleon appeared to incarnate quite precisely the archetypal synthesis of Prometheus and Mars, so did Leonardo appear to be an ideal embodiment of Prometheus combined with Venus—not only his singular artistic genius, but also his many technical innovations in the arts, his theory and practice of what he called the "science of painting," and more generally his lifelong synthesis of artistic and scientific discovery. I noticed too that a number of other masters of artistic beauty were born with Venus and Uranus in major aspect, such as Raphael, Rembrandt, and Monet.

An interesting case of a "compromise formation" of Venus–Uranus and Mars–Uranus was that of Michelangelo, the third of the High Renaissance triumvirate with Leonardo and Raphael. While Michelangelo was born with Venus in an important midpoint configuration with Uranus (VE/UR = JU 1°16'), the more conspicuously prominent planet in this regard was Mars, since he had a Mars–Sun conjunction in a trine with Uranus. Here I thought of Michelangelo's characteristic choice of subjects, as in his two greatest sculptures, *David* and *Moses*, both of whom were specifically martial liberators (Mars with Prometheus). Although obviously many other natal factors are relevant to the character of an artist's work, I thought it interesting that, considering the greater emphasis on Venus and the Moon in the charts of Leonardo and Raphael, very generally speaking the art of both of the latter two painters was indeed more consistently focused on feminine beauty, on the tender and soft, on virgins, maidens, madonnas, and angels, with even their male figures tending to exhibit a certain gentle beauty; while by contrast, Michelangelo's art was typically more masculine both in choice of subject and in tone—thus the muscular assertiveness and strength not only of David and Moses, and of the Sistine ceiling's Adam and God the Creator, but even of many of his female figures as well. This archetypal difference was also evident when the three artists treated the same Promethean figure, as in the serene and caring Christs of Leonardo's *Last Supper* and Raphael's *La Disputa del Sacramento* compared with the angry militant Christ of Michelangelo's *Last Judgment*.

In the case of other artists and writers born with major Venus–Uranus aspects, I regularly noticed a highly specific linkage of the Venus and Prometheus archetypes in the basic themes of their work. With Shelley, who was born with Uranus in major aspect to Venus (in a triple conjunction with the Sun), the figure of Prometheus in his *Prometheus Unbound* strove to bring a reign of freedom, love, and beauty to humanity. This explicit linking of Promethean rebellion and liberation to Venusian beauty and love was also visible in Richard Wagner (as in *Tristan und Isolde*), he too born with Uranus in major aspect to both Venus and the Sun. Also in Wagner could be seen the theme of liberation through art, as well as radical artistic innovation, again logical results of combining the Prometheus and Venus archetypes. William Blake was born with Venus and Uranus in major aspect, he too displaying an emphatic association of art and revolution, a belief in spiritual liberation through art and sensuous experience, and, in his own innovative method of illuminated engraving, a direct linking of artistic expression with technical invention. I was also struck by the fact that the one philosopher I noticed who was born with these two planets in major aspect was Schopenhauer, whose central doctrine held art and aesthetic contemplation to be the principal area of human experience that allows liberation from the bondage of existence.

Given Venus's association with romantic love and Prometheus's with freedom and rebellion, I was interested in the ways in which Venus–Uranus aspects would be correlated with romantic love's breaking out of conventional limitations and structures, as in extramarital relationships or those otherwise condemned by social opinion or parental authority. I found that this unconventional romance was an extremely characteristic theme of the art, and often the personal lives as well, of not only Shelley and Wagner, but also Tolstoy, Dostoevsky, Chekhov, Verdi, Feydeau, Pasternak, and T. H. White, all of whom were born with Venus and Uranus in major aspect. This Prometheus–Venus theme was also markedly characteristic of the plays and poetry of Shakespeare, and the best estimates for his birth date (21–23 April 1564) coincide with a period when Venus and Uranus were in close opposition. Two other themes appropriate to the synthesis of Venus and Prometheus—the sudden unexpected awakening of new love, and redemption through love—figured prominently in most of these artists' work as well.

An especially interesting category was that of those born with major aspects between Uranus and Mercury. Given the latter's association with the intellect and communication, I here checked for correlations between natal Mercury–Uranus aspects and persons noted specifically for their exceptional independence of mind, intellectual brilliance, sudden insights and inventiveness, revolutionary ideas, extraordinary powers of communication, command of language, innovative or otherwise unusual relationship to language and communication, special achievements in writing and literature, and so on. Again I found a number of remarkable correlations. Five giants of German thought and literature—Goethe, Schiller, Hegel, Nietzsche, and Heidegger—were all born with this combination of planets in major aspect. Among the leading figures of the Enlightenment, Voltaire, Diderot, Hume, and Franklin all had it. Among the intellectual architects of the American Revolution and Constitution, both Madison and Jefferson, as well as Franklin, were born with it.

Abraham Lincoln and Charles Darwin, born on the same day (12 February 1809), both had it—both distinguished for their intellectual brilliance and independence as well as their powers of communication in the service of major revolutions. Among historians, both Spengler and Toynbee had it. So also other notably original thinkers such as the British polymaths Alfred North Whitehead, Bertrand Russell, and John Maynard Keynes. Among psychoanalysts, Freud had it, as did Otto Rank, Melanie Klein, Wilhelm Reich, Fritz Perls, and James Hillman—all rebels against the orthodox psychoanalytic fold (as was, indeed, Freud himself).

Limited space does not permit here a detailed discussion of the relevant archetypal characteristics for each person cited (though these are generally self-evident), but the case of Benjamin Franklin can be used as a good example of how the biographical themes of a person born with a major Mercury–Uranus aspect can express, in diverse and yet archetypally very specific forms, the combining of Mercury and Prometheus: thus Franklin's many practical inventions (Franklin stove, lightning rod, bifocal glasses), his pioneering electrical experiments and theories, his lifelong curiosity, ingenuity, and wit, his career as a printer and his famous Poor Richard almanacs with their pithy aphorisms, his founding of such new institutions in the colonies as a philosophical society, a library system, and an educational academy, his administering the colonial postal service, his long service as mediator between the American colonies and France and England, and his role in drafting the Declaration of Independence and United States Constitution. The Promethean component in all of this was nicely suggested in the famous epigram by Turgot: "He snatched the lightning from the skies and the sceptre from tyrants."

When I looked more specifically into the realm of literature, I found that all four of England's preeminent women novelists of the nineteenth century —Jane Austen, Charlotte and Emily Brontë, and George Eliot—were born with Mercury in major aspect to Uranus. Also among great English novelists, Charles Dickens and William Thackeray both had it, as did Henry Fielding a century earlier, and, in America a century later, William Faulkner. In France, Balzac was born with it, as was Proust.

Also in French literature, I checked to see whether Mercury–Uranus aspects would be associated with the avant-garde and radical innovations in poetry. Here I found that Baudelaire, Verlaine, Rimbaud, and Laforgue—perhaps the four nineteenth-century French poets most representative of this tendency—all were born with those planets in major aspect. So also was their influential successor in modernist English poetry, T. S. Eliot.

Checking further the use of language in unconventional or eccentric ways, as in innovations or experiments with syntax, punctuation, typography, and the sound and meaning of words, I found that both Gertrude Stein and e.e. cummings were born with Mercury and Uranus in major aspect. Similarly, given Uranus's association with the unexpected and anomalous, I thought that Mercury–Uranus aspects might be relevant to those whose work was marked by sudden unexpected changes of meaning and the defiance of conventional logic, by an element of the absurd: I found that Kafka, Sartre, Genet, and Beckett were all born with these planets in major aspect. So also was Jacques Derrida (avant-garde literary criticism and philosophy, rebellion against traditional academic standards, unconventional logic and syntax, a penchant for neologisms). And so too Oscar Wilde, master of paradox and the play of language, and remarkable as well for his epigrammatic brilliance (a classic Mercury–Prometheus *bon mot*, Wilde at the United States Customs: "I have nothing to declare but my genius"). Niels Bohr, whose principle of complementarity remains the paradigm of scientific paradox, was born with this configuration as well (compare Bohr's dictum, "The opposite of a great truth is another great truth," with Wilde's, "A truth in art is that whose contradictory is also true," and with the dialectical synthesis of opposites in the philosophy of Hegel).

I also noticed that an extraordinary number of persons born with major Mercury–Uranus aspects possessed an unusual aptitude for mastering many languages. Among others, one could single out Jefferson, Goethe, Hegel, Baudelaire, Nietzsche, Freud, Eliot, Beckett, Heidegger, and Hillman. Jefferson, for example, knew Greek, Latin, French, Italian, Spanish, and Anglo-Saxon. Friedrich Engels, born with the conjunction of Mercury and Uranus, knew twenty-four languages. The nineteenth-century scholar-explorer Sir Richard Burton, also born with these planets in major aspect, knew twenty-five languages (forty, if one includes dialects). Noam Chomsky, who revolutionized modern linguistics itself, was born with Mercury–Uranus in major aspect as well.

Equally notable was the number of persons in this group—indeed most of those cited above—who were well-known for coining new words or for employing existing words in a novel, unexpected fashion. And in general I observed throughout this category a marked tendency for the use of, or the concern with, puns, double entendres, linguistic and semantic sleights of hand, twists of meaning through translation, word play of all kinds—a tricksterism with language precisely appropriate to the archetypal combination of Prometheus with Mercury—whether as a characteristic method of argument (Heidegger, Sartre, Derrida), as an important stylistic trait (Wilde, Nietzsche, Hillman, most of the cited poets), as both a subject and a method of psychological analysis (Freud), or simply as a personal habit in conversation or private letters (as with Kepler and T. S. Eliot).

One person who seemed to exemplify, indeed epitomize, many of the characteristics cited above for Mercury–Uranus natal aspects was James Joyce: literary genius, stylistic originality, mastery of many languages, unprecedented word play and linguistic experimentation, obsession with puns—the trickster with words. In Joyce's case, as in many others not noted in this brief discussion, I found that this archetypal combination was found not as a major aspect between the corresponding planets, but as a significant midpoint configuration. Thus with Joyce I found that he was born with Mercury at the exact square of the Sun/Uranus midpoint (0°36'). (Here I thought also of Joseph Campbell, born with both Mercury and the Sun in square to Uranus, whose first book, *A Skeleton Key to Finnegan's Wake*, provided an ingenious decoding of Joyce's final and most radically experimental and linguistically multileveled work.)

More generally, I found that the Mercury–Uranus configuration seemed to occur with unusual frequency among men and women of letters—particularly literary critics—whose intellectual character and work closely fit what one would expect of the Mercury–Prometheus archetypal combination: i.e., intellectual brilliance, highly original literary perspectives and theories, championing of artistic innovation and revolutionary movements in literature. Even among those already cited one could mention as examples of this tendency such influential critics as Gertrude Stein, T. S. Eliot, Sartre, and Derrida (and, in previous centuries, Voltaire, Goethe, Schiller, and Wilde). The leading American man of letters in this century, Edmund Wilson, was born with this configuration, as was H. L. Mencken, noted for his iconoclastic cultural criticism, untrammeled wit, and inventive language, as well as for being the leading authority on American English and an influential supporter of innovative writers. So too Maxwell Perkins, the legendary editor for many of America's most original writers in the first half of the century (Fitzgerald, Hemingway, Wolfe). Harold Bloom, the leading contemporary American critic whose principal theory addressed the workings of the Promethean–Oedipal impulse in the literary tradition, also was born with this configuration—which, interestingly, he shared with Jacques Derrida who was born four days later. (Bloom's main literary theory involves the idea that the literary creator is compelled to "steal" and transform for his or her own purposes the work of predecessors in the tradition, and that the continuum of artistic originality is based fundamentally on such acts of rebellion and appropriation.) In addition, three other eminent contemporary men of letters, V. S. Pritchett, Anthony Burgess, and John Updike, were all born with Mercury and Uranus in major aspect (conjunction in all three cases, as with T. S. Eliot). The paradigmatic English man of letters, Samuel Johnson, was born with Mercury (and Sun) in conjunction to the Jupiter/Uranus midpoint.

Given Mercury's archetypal association with movement as well as communication, I found it of interest that Mercury–Uranus natal aspects occurred frequently with persons in whom communication was expressed *through* the act of movement in highly creative and unorthodox ways. For example, Charlie Chaplin, Buster Keaton, and Marcel Marceau all were born with major Mercury–Uranus aspects, all three being geniuses of movement with unusual styles of communication involving various characteristics of the trickster: extraordinary cleverness and inventiveness, levity and wit, surprise and unexpected timing, rapidity of movement and repeated sudden shifts of meaning.

In a further variation on Mercury–Prometheus themes, I found that Alfred Hitchcock and Agatha Christie, both noted for the ingenuity of their sudden and startling plot twists, unexpected shifts of meaning, and surprise endings, also were born with these two planets in major aspect. So too was the world chess champion Bobby Fischer, the youngest player in the world to attain the rank of grand master (age fifteen), whose victories typically resulted from a strategy of sudden surprise moves.

Because of Mercury's closeness to the Sun, I found much overlap in this category with those who were born with the Sun and Uranus in aspect. For example, Galileo, Freud, William James, and Jefferson all had both Mercury and the Sun in major aspect to Uranus at birth. In these latter cases I noted that, though writing was not their principal concern, all four of these men communicated their ideas with exceptional literary skill and originality of expression (for example, Freud's being awarded the Goethe Prize for literature, Jefferson's eloquent Declaration of Independence, etc.).

Another interesting case was that of Kepler, who was born with Uranus in a multiple conjunction that included not only the Sun and Mercury but also Venus. Here I recalled the fact that Kepler's scientific efforts were impelled above all by Platonic and

Pythagorean principles that were specifically aesthetic in character, including his belief in "the harmony of the spheres." As those familiar with his biography and the history of science can attest, this conjunction at Kepler's birth archetypally corresponded very closely to the fact that in Kepler's life the intellectual (Mercury), the aesthetic (Venus), and the revolutionary (Prometheus–Uranus) were all singularly conjoined and inseparable.

In general I found that Mercury–Uranus natal aspects occurred rather frequently among unusually innovative or independent-minded scientists. Besides Galileo, Kepler, Franklin, Darwin, James, Freud, Whitehead, and Bohr already mentioned, more recent figures born with this configuration include Jean Piaget, Norbert Wiener, Francis Crick, James Watson, Richard Feynman, and Stephen Hawking, as well as Hans Eysenck. Also, considering Thomas Kuhn's highly original analysis of the nature of scientific revolution itself, I was struck by the fact that he too was born with Mercury and Uranus in major aspect.

Sometimes the impulse associated with the Prometheus archetype seems to express itself in a life in only one specific area, as if this were the only open channel. I found the case of Franz Kafka suggestive in this regard, with his exact square of Uranus to Mercury. In his diaries, Kafka repeatedly described that it was *only during the activity of writing* that he felt any degree of personal freedom and excitement. The rest of his life he experienced as an inexplicable eternity of psychological imprisonment, self-torture, and physical debilitation (these associated with his Saturn–Pluto and Mars–Neptune conjunctions). In his writings, however, created in unpredictable flashes of inspiration, Kafka revolutionized twentieth-century fiction. Appropriately, he wrote a short story entitled "Prometheus" in which he recounts four variations of the myth in his own, Kafkaesque fashion. In the final version, the gods, the eagle, and Prometheus himself forget the meaning of the whole affair; this unexpected twist of absurdity to the legend seemed especially appropriate for Uranus square Mercury.

Mercury was exactly conjoined to Venus at Kafka's birth, and thus he also had Uranus square Venus. This latter combination seemed relevant to Kafka's series of unstable relationships with women, love affairs repeatedly broken off just before marriage. Of special interest in light of this three-planet complex of Mercury–Venus–Uranus was the fact that Kafka's ambivalence and unpredictability in this area was explicitly related to his fear that a relationship with a woman would destroy his writing; also, these affairs both sporadically inspired and interrupted his literary efforts.

This brief overview could be extended indefinitely with further examples and variations, but these are perhaps sufficient to suggest something of the nature of the evidence I first encountered in studying possible correlations between the archetype of Prometheus and the planet Uranus in natal aspect to the inner planets. Many of these apparent correspondences were based on intuitively striking commonalities that did not lend themselves readily to "objective" evaluation. Generally speaking, the recognition of archetypes is too complex and ambiguous, too dependent on a psychologically perceptive and culturally informed sensibility capable of recognizing subtle patterns and nuances, to be fruitfully subjected to any purely quantitative form of analysis. The task facing the person engaged in this form of research is closer in nature to the task facing the historian, the biographer, and the depth psychologist, rather than the statistician.

Yet I found the many correspondences impressive, particularly the apt archetypal differentiations between the various planetary combinations. It was as if each Uranus aspect reflected the "liberation" of a specific archetypal impulse—Prometheus liberating the Mercury impulse of ideas and language and communication, for example, or freeing the Venus impulse of art and beauty and love, or liberating the Mars impulse of assertiveness and militant aggression. Conversely, those same archetypes could be understood as the specific channels through which the Promethean impulse of creative innovation, rebellion, unpredictability, and individualism was particularly expressed. Each natal aspect between Uranus and another planet seemed to represent a distinct mutual activation of the corresponding archetypes.

And perhaps it would also be well to recall here something mentioned in an earlier part of this essay: namely, that the investigation of significant cultural figures is valuable not because they alone were born with the aspects in question, which they were not, nor because these aspects in any way guarantee, as it were, such prominence or accomplishment, but rather because the lives and characters of such individuals express specific archetypal characteristics in a manner that is especially conspicuous and publicly assessable. Such figures are useful for research not because they are typical, but because they are paradigmatic.

Natal Uranus Aspects Cited in Text

Napoleon Bonaparte	0°33'	Uranus trine Mars
V. I. Lenin	5°24'†	Uranus square Mars
Mao Tse-tung	11°50'†	Uranus conjunct Mars (MA/UR = JU, 1°11')
Friedrich Nietzsche	5°37	Uranus opposite Mars
Leonardo da Vinci	1°36'	Uranus sextile Venus
Raphael	7°29'	Uranus trine Venus
Rembrandt	7°46'†	Uranus conjunct Venus

Claude Monet	4°40'†	Uranus square Venus
Michelangelo	3°48'	Uranus trine Mars
Percy Bysshe Shelley	6°20'	Uranus conjunct Venus
Richard Wagner	3°57'	Uranus opposite Venus
William Blake	0°15'	Uranus sextile Venus
Arthur Schopenhauer	6°48'	Uranus trine Venus
Leo Tolstoy	5°20'†	Uranus opposite Venus
Fyodor Dostoevsky	0°14'†	Uranus conjunct Venus
Anton Chekhov	4°06'†	Uranus square Venus
Guiseppe Verdi	2°51'	Uranus conjunct Venus
Georges Feydeau	2°13'†	Uranus opposite Venus
Boris Pasternak	6°45'†	Uranus trine Venus
T. H. White	4°20'†	Uranus opposite Venus
William Shakespeare	5°30'†	Uranus opposite Venus
Johannes Kepler	9°55'	Uranus conjunct Venus
Franz Kafka	0°00†	Uranus square Venus
J. W. von Goethe	7°09'	Uranus opposite Mercury (ME = SU/UR, 1°02')
Friedrich von Schiller	6°30'†	Uranus trine Mercury
Georg W. F. Hegel	1°40'†	Uranus trine Mercury
Friedrich Nietzsche	0°36'	Uranus opposite Mercury
Martin Heidegger	7°50'†	Uranus conjunct Mercury
Voltaire	1°30'†	Uranus opposite Mercury
Denis Diderot	10°15'†	Uranus conjunct Mercury (UR = ME/JU 0°10')
David Hume	6°00'†	Uranus square Mercury
Benjamin Franklin	5°30'†	Uranus opposite Mercury
James Madison	2°26'	Uranus conjunct Mercury
Thomas Jefferson	0°20'†	Uranus sextile Mercury
Abraham Lincoln	0°40'†	Uranus trine Mercury
Charles Darwin	0°20'†	Uranus trine Mercury
Oswald Spengler	0°57'	Uranus square Mercury
Arnold J. Toynbee	6°30'†	Uranus opposite Mercury

Alfred North Whitehead	0°40'†	Uranus square Mercury
Bertrand Russell	5°27'	Uranus square Mercury
John Maynard Keynes	0°48'†	Uranus square Mercury
Sigmund Freud	7°12'	Uranus conjunct Mercury
Otto Rank	1°58'†	Uranus trine Mercury
Melanie Klein	1°54'†	Uranus opposite Mercury
Wilhelm Reich	3°15'†	Uranus trine Mercury
Fritz Perls	5°46'†	Uranus square Mercury
James Hillman	5°43'	Uranus conjunct Mercury
Jane Austen	2°22'	Uranus opposite Mercury
Charlotte Brontë	5°58'†	Uranus trine Mercury
Emily Brontë	4°13'†	Uranus trine Mercury
George Eliot	6°46'	Uranus conjunct Mercury
Charles Dickens	0°53'†	Uranus sextile Mercury
William Thackeray	3°00'†	Uranus trine Mercury
Henry Fielding	6°57'†	Uranus square Mercury
William Faulkner	0°10'†	Uranus sextile Mercury
Honore de Balzac	6°21'	Uranus trine Mercury
Marcel Proust	8°44'	Uranus conjunct Mercury
Charles Baudelaire	5°45'	Uranus square Mercury
Paul Verlaine	0°51'	Uranus conjunct Mercury
Arthur Rimbaud	3°21'	Uranus opposite Mercury
Jules Laforgue	1°56'†	Uranus sextile Mercury
T. S. Eliot	9°49'	Uranus conjunct Mercury
Gertrude Stein	6°20'	Uranus opposite Mercury
e.e. cummings	0°48'†	Uranus conjunct Mercury
Franz Kafka	0°03'†	Uranus square Mercury
Jean-Paul Sartre	5°55'	Uranus opposite Mercury
Jean Genet	7°41'	Uranus conjunct Mercury
Samuel Beckett	0°16'†	Uranus square Mercury
Jacques Derrida	6°58'†	Uranus square Mercury
Oscar Wilde	2°13'	Uranus opposite Mercury
Niels Bohr	3°42'†	Uranus conjunct Mercury

Friedrich Engels	5°14'†	Uranus conjunct Mercury
Sir Richard Burton	5°52'	Uranus square Mercury
Noam Chomsky	5°54'†	Uranus trine Mercury
Johannes Kepler	3°06'	Uranus conjunct Mercury
Joseph Campbell	6°08'	Uranus square Mercury
Edmund Wilson	4°14'†	Uranus opposite Mercury
H. L. Mencken	6°42'	Uranus conjunct Mercury
Maxwell Perkins	2°22'†	Uranus conjunct Mercury
Harold Bloom	1°08'†	Uranus square Mercury
V. S. Pritchett	8°21'†	Uranus conjunct Mercury
Anthony Burgess	7°28'†	Uranus conjunct Mercury
John Updike	2°53'†	Uranus conjunct Mercury
Charlie Chaplin	1°49'	Uranus opposite Mercury
Buster Keaton	10°55'†	Uranus conjunct Mercury
Marcel Marceau	0°37'†	Uranus conjunct Mercury
Alfred Hitchcock	3°04'†	Uranus square Mercury
Agatha Christie	9°42'†	Uranus conjunct Mercury
Bobby Fischer	3°06'	Uranus square Mercury
Galileo Galilei	5°01'	Uranus square Mercury
William James	4°12'†	Uranus sextile Mercury
Jean Piaget	5°52'†	Uranus square Mercury
Norbert Wiener	2°12'	Uranus conjunct Mercury
Francis Crick	5°58'†	Uranus trine Mercury
James Watson	10°56'†	Uranus conjunct Mercury (UR = SU/ME 1°40')
Richard Feynman	2°58'†	Uranus sextile Mercury
Stephen Hawking	1°30'†	Uranus trine Mercury
Hans Eysenck	0°58'	Uranus conjunct Mercury
Thomas Kuhn	6°40'†	Uranus trine Mercury

† ± < 1° (date of birth only)

IV

PROMETHEUS AND ASTROLOGY

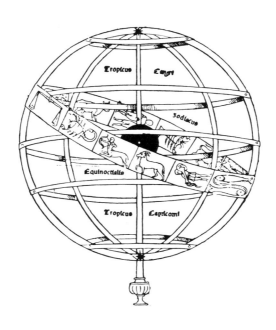

Not the least of the many unexpected rewards permitted by the study of astrology is the extraordinary aesthetic satisfaction it so consistently affords. With its seemingly unending disclosure of elegant archetypal patternings synchronously coinciding with corresponding planetary alignments, astrology would appear to have been designed by the cosmos, as it were, to bring forth a certain appreciative awe in witness of this inconceivably complex orchestration. And contrary to the assumption of many unversed in the study, the more rigorous the intellectual care brought to the astrological investigation, the more profound the resulting intellectual pleasure. Yet it is the nature of astrological correlations that they demand a different kind of epistemology from that employed by the conventional scientific mind—an eye for multidimensional archetypal structures, an openness to the possibility of meaningful coincidence, a willingness to transcend limited assumptions about the nature of reality. Such correlations are more readily visible to the epistemologically flexible mind—more accessible, one might say, to the mind of a Sherlock Holmes, rather than to the more staid cognitive style of the Scotland Yard establishment.

It is thus appropriate that the creator of Sherlock Holmes, Sir Arthur Conan Doyle, was born with a close Sun–Uranus conjunction. Holmes's genius, much like the modus operandi of the astrologer, consists in his observing a variety of minute data that the average person would dismiss or ignore, and detecting in those scattered traces an underlying pattern, a coherent narrative of compelling meaning—a transcendent myth, in a sense. He sees through apparently meaningless and haphazard facts to leap to a new level of comprehension. This unexpected resolution liberates both Holmes's client from a dangerous predicament and the reader from the dramatic tension created by the previously inexplicable series of events. Holmes's passion for ingeniously deciphering material clues is a Promethean quest to liberate meaning from the imprisonment of ignorance. One of the most original and vividly realized characters in English literature, Holmes is a superb embodiment of the Uranus–Prometheus impulse, a cerebral virtuoso of eccentric brilliance with unorthodox but supremely effective methods of mental processing.[1]

Holmes regularly employed the psychoactive drug cocaine to enhance his meditations, against Dr. Watson's concerned medical warnings, and we may recall that that other legendary user of cocaine, Sigmund Freud, also had a close Sun–Uranus conjunction. Many of cocaine's characteristic effects are markedly Promethean: the sudden stimulation of the mental processes, the electrifying sense of intellectual acuity, a technological synthesis that produces an unexpected and brief expansion of awareness. Of note is the transit Freud had at the time of his initial and most intensive cocaine experiments, 1884–85, when he wrote his classic papers on the psychopharmacology of cocaine: his natal Sun–Uranus conjunction was then being exactly conjoined by transiting Neptune (associated with, inter alia, drugs, altered states of consciousness, transcendence, escapism, and addictive tendencies). This correlation is of interest in itself, but in what can perhaps best be described as a most singular coincidence, during the years of Sherlock Holmes's fictional use of cocaine, 1887–90, Arthur Conan Doyle had the identical once-in-a-lifetime transit that occurred in Freud's chart during *his* cocaine episode: transiting Neptune conjunct natal Sun and Uranus.

There are further parallels between the two geniuses. Their peculiarly penetrating intellects could focus with obsessive concentration on whatever subject gripped their attention and, from sheer intensity of mental energy, move toward the solution of almost impossibly opaque mysteries. Both Doyle and Freud had prominent Mercury–Pluto configurations (Doyle with Mercury conjunct Pluto 2°09', Freud with Sun conjunct the Mercury/Pluto midpoint 0°03'), perhaps the archetypal combination most conducive to producing an intensely penetrating mind. The extreme intensity of Pluto seems to compel the Mercury principle of intellect into its most forceful manifestation, creating an overwhelming mental drive to penetrate below the superficial to get to the root of the matter. Reading Freud's analysis of "The Dream of Irma's Injection," for instance, reminds one strongly of a painstaking Holmesian analysis of obscure clues at the scene of a crime.[2]

Mercury–Pluto also appears to be associated with a pronounced intellectual concern with the underworld, both criminal and unconscious—the intensive study of the mysterious, of the depths, of the instincts, of crime and sin, of murderous emotions, of the dark and hidden recesses of human nature—again, both Freud's and Holmes's special area of expertise. A redemptive element in the archetypal natures of both Prometheus and Pluto is suggested by the fact that not only were these two men able to detect hidden motivations and dark meanings behind seemingly innocent actions or words, they were also equally capable of recognizing genuine innocence behind apparently damning evidence, whether it was Holmes's ingenious restoration of a wrongly accused client or Freud's therapeutic rescue of a neurotic patient. With the intensity of concentration and focused intellectual power of Mercury–Pluto combined with a Promethean impulse for daring experiment and capacity for sudden liberating breakthroughs, both Freud and Holmes were singularly equipped for their mental endeavors. In view of these two geniuses *nonpareil*, it is difficult to imagine a more formidable intelligence than that of a person born with both Sun–Uranus and Mercury–Pluto in such powerful aspect.[3]

Thus specific archetypes and archetypal combinations seem to manifest themselves with a suggestive thematic consistency in individuals with similar configurations in their natal charts. We see this in the remarkable case of *Thus Spoke Zarathustra*. In this instance, Nietzsche's work inspired Richard Strauss, the last great German Romantic composer, to write a tone poem of the same name which in its first majestic measures gives powerful expression to the Promethean archetypal impulse. Strauss had Uranus in close conjunction to his Sun at birth. These same measures were then used by Stanley Kubrick to introduce the highly Promethean film *2001: A Space Odyssey*, with themes of evolutionary breakthrough, "The Dawn of Man," technological genius, radical consciousness transformation, the future birth of a new form of human being, and so forth. Kubrick was born with Uranus in close trine to his Sun. Thus the Zarathustra–Prometheus impulse can be recognized manifesting successively in the creations of individuals with Uranus prominently aspected in their natal charts: Nietzsche wrote the book, Strauss gave it musical form, and Kubrick gave it cinematic expression.[4]

The widespread use of psychedelics as tools for the transformation of consciousness—a major factor in the 1960s revolution—is an apt example of Prometheus's fire, containing the elements of technological invention (the chemical synthesis of LSD) and scientific breakthrough (the discovery of its power as a psychotherapeutic catalyst), as well as sudden unexpected reality shifts and spiritual awakenings, with the overthrow of the controlling ego resulting in a liberation of the transpersonal unconscious and a radical expansion of awareness. Timothy Leary and Richard Alpert (now Ram Dass), the two men whose experiments at Harvard in the early 1960s helped initiate the psychedelic revolution, were both born with Uranus in close major aspect to the Sun —as also was William James, the American psychologist and philosopher whose *Varieties of Religious Experience* at the beginning of the century first pointed to the importance of psychedelic substances for exploring the nature of reality and the psyche.[5]

The Uranus–Pluto Cycle

But archetypally patterned correlations like these take on greater significance when we find them on a larger historical scale, revealing the remarkably consistent coincidence of major cultural phenomena with the great cycles of the outer planets. The Uranus–Pluto conjunction of the 1960s was discussed at the end of Part I of this essay, and here we recall the extent to which the various individual Promethean qualities and phenomena just alluded to were part of much larger cultural trends at that time—the rebellion against established structures of all kinds, the intense intellectual adventurousness and restlessness of the era, the radical consciousness transformation, the titanic technological advances into the space age, the general atmosphere of revolution on all fronts—all very much characteristic of the period 1960–72 when Uranus and Pluto were within 15° of exact conjunction. Yet this correlation becomes more remarkable when seen against the backdrop of the great sequence of Uranus–Pluto alignments through the centuries.

For example, we find that Uranus and Pluto were in opposition during the decade of the French Revolution—centered in the early 1790s and within 15° from 1787 to 1798—a period whose character was conspicuously similar to that of the 1960s. Here again was the tremendous empowerment of the Promethean revolutionary impulse, bringing the profound social and political transformation of not only France but of all Europe. Here again was the prodigious energy and activism of the period, the overwhelming and multiform impulse to rebellion, reform, and restless experiment, the revolt against oppression, the general impulse toward "radicalization," the suddenly empowered will to construct a new world. As in the 1960s there was in the 1790s the assertion of new freedoms in virtually every realm—social, political, economic, intellectual, artistic, religious. The word "revolution" itself, so often heard in the 1960s and so central to that era's spirit, first came into wide use in its present meaning of sudden radical change in the 1790s.

Similarly, the conjunction that followed the 1787–98 opposition took place from 1845 to 1856, coinciding precisely with the great wave of revolutions that swept through Europe in 1848–49—the very next period that was comparable in character to that of the French Revolution. Once again there was the sudden eruption of a collective revolutionary impulse affecting an entire continent, bringing near-simultaneous revolutions and insurrections in almost every capital in Europe—Paris, Berlin, Vienna, Budapest, Prague, Rome, Milan, Dresden, Baden. We also see this same sustained mass eruption of Promethean energy during the Uranus–Pluto

opposition of 1643 to 1653 (that immediately preceded that of the French Revolution), which quite
precisely coincided with England's Puritan Revolution or Civil War of that decade (referred to in its
own century as the Great Rebellion), which was in
turn part of a larger wave of revolutions and rebellions that swept Europe at that time. Here again was
the collective emergence of a many-sided impulse to
make over the world in radically new ways, erupting
simultaneously in many countries—a phenomenon
that indeed has puzzled historians for generations.

The Jupiter–Uranus Cycle

A more frequent activation of the Prometheus
impulse in the cultural psyche regularly occurs in
coincidence with the Jupiter–Uranus cycle, with the
two planets conjoining approximately every fourteen years. When Jupiter and a second planet enter
into alignment, Jupiter's archetypal influence seems
to be one of magnifying and supporting the second
planetary archetype—expanding it, granting it success, bringing it to fruition. Also, perhaps because
of Jupiter's archetypal relation to the area of high
culture, Jupiter–Uranus alignments often coincide
with simultaneous individual breakthroughs in such
fields as philosophy, science, literature, and the arts.

For example, it was during the Jupiter–Uranus

conjunction of 1609–1610 that Galileo first turned his telescope to the heavens and published his historic discoveries in *Sidereus Nuncius*, and that Kepler's equally epochal discovery of the first two laws of planetary motion (stating that the planets moved in elliptical orbits with speeds based on equal areas swept out in equal times) appeared in *Astronomia Nova*, thereby resolving the problem of the planets that had dominated Western planetary astronomy for two millennia. In one of the great coincidences in the history of science, Kepler and Galileo independently made public within a few months of each other their separate discoveries suddenly confirming the Copernican theory of the solar system. The combination of the two events provided the scientific world with a concurrence of evidence that effectively substantiated the heliocentric theory, gradually brought the latter to widespread public attention, and laid the foundations for the eventual success of the Copernican revolution. Jupiter and Uranus were in close conjunction (0–5°) at the time of both publications, having been within 15° of each other during the fourteen-month period from April 1609 to June 1610.

Similarly, Jupiter and Uranus were in conjunction during the fourteen-month period from November 1899 through December 1900. It has often been pointed out that during this short period at the turn of the twentieth century, two of the century's most important intellectual revolutions, psychoanalysis and quantum physics, were born. The former was first brought to public notice at this time with the publication in Vienna of Freud's *Interpretation of Dreams*, while during this same period Max Planck announced his discovery that radiant energy is emitted or absorbed in discrete quanta, as well as his fundamental formulation of the quantum theory, in two meetings of the German Physical Society in Berlin, thereby initiating the twentieth-century revolution of modern physics.

Appropriate to its own theory, quantum physics has not progressed in continuous fashion but rather has developed with two major quantum leaps: one at its birth in 1900 with Planck, and the second, its coming to maturity, in 1927–28. Jupiter and Uranus were again conjunct during the extraordinary period in 1927–28 when Niels Bohr, Werner Heisenberg, and their colleagues culminated the quantum physics revolution begun by Planck, working both individually and then in interaction at the historic October 1927 Solvay congress in Brussels. The resulting synthesis was, in the words of the intellectual leader of the congress, Bohr, the result of "a singularly fruitful cooperation of a whole generation of physicists," including Erwin Schrodinger, Max Born, Louis de Broglie, Wolfgang Pauli, Paul Dirac, as well as Planck and Heisenberg. It has been said that in 1927 the pace of discovery in theoretical physics was probably greater than in any other year in the history of science. During the period of this conjunction, from March 1927 through April 1928, both of the two major revolutionary axioms of quantum mechanics, Heisenberg's Principle of Indeterminacy and Bohr's Principle of Complementarity, were formulated and made public. In addition, it was during this same conjunction in 1927 that the Belgian astrophysicist Georges Lemaître first proposed the Big Bang theory of the origin of the universe.

Jupiter and Uranus were also in conjunction at the time of the famous series of events leading to the first public announcement of the theory of evolution by Charles Darwin and Alfred Russel Wallace in July 1858. Although Darwin had privately formulated the theory of evolution in 1838 during his Uranus-trine-Uranus transit, he did not make his findings public for over twenty years, instead gradually accumulating evidence and developing the theory in relative isolation. Then on 18 June 1858, he unexpectedly received from Wallace, who was then in the Malay Archipelago, a letter containing a statement of the theory of evolution which Wallace had conceived independently in virtually identical form. As a result of this letter and the urgings of Darwin's colleagues, a joint paper by Darwin and Wallace was read before the Linnean Society of London on 1 July 1858, announcing the theory to the world. Immediately afterward, still during this conjunction, Darwin commenced writing his magnum opus, *The Origin of Species*, the foundational work of modern biology.

Many other examples of major scientific breakthroughs occurring in coincidence with Jupiter–Uranus conjunctions and oppositions could be cited: Newton's invention of the concept of universal gravitation and writing of the *Principia* in 1685–86, the crucial experiments by Lavoisier and Priestley that led to the birth of modern chemistry in 1775–76, Dalton's first statement of the atomic theory of matter in 1803, Faraday's historic experiments demonstrating his discovery of electromagnetic induction in 1831, Maxwell's landmark paper setting forth the theory of electromagnetic fields in 1865, Mendel's announcement of his discovery of the laws of heredity in the same year, and so forth.

When we turn from the sciences to the arts, we find an equally remarkable coincidence of Jupiter–Uranus alignments with significant Promethean events. In the field of music, for example, Beethoven's *Eroica*, his Third Symphony, the most explicitly Promethean work in the history of classical music—supremely revolutionary in spirit and conception, as well as in historical impact—was composed in the summer and fall of 1803 under the same Jupiter–Uranus that coincided with Dalton's breakthrough in chemistry. The one work of the later nineteenth century that ranks with the *Eroica* in terms of musical revolution, Wagner's *Tristan und Isolde*, was composed in 1858, under the same Jupiter–Uranus conjunction that coincided with the announcement of the theory of evolution by Darwin and Wallace. Moreover, looking backward in time for that composition which most fully anticipated the *Eroica*, namely Mozart's *Jupiter* Symphony, we find that it was written under the Jupiter–Uranus conjunction of 1788–89, the one that immediately preceded the conjunction coincident with the *Eroica*.

Similarly, in the history of film, the three consecutive Jupiter–Uranus conjunctions that occurred during the cinema's first fifty years exactly coincided with the three films one would immediately think of as those which had the most significant impact on the evolution of the cinema. Thus D. W. Griffith's *Birth of a Nation*, widely considered the single most influential work in the history of film, its many technical and aesthetic innovations establishing the vocabulary of the new art, was made during the Jupiter–Uranus conjunction of 1914 (released early 1915). The immediately following conjunction of 1927–28 exactly coincided with the film with synchronized sound that revolutionized the motion picture industry, *The Jazz Singer* with Al Jolson, its celebrated premiere in October 1927 (the same month as the Bohr–Heisenberg Solvay physics conference) marking the birth of the sound era. And the next conjunction of 1940–41 (July 1940 to August 1941) precisely coincided with Orson Welles's *Citizen Kane* (premiere May 1941), a great landmark in the history of sound film, its mastery of many technical and artistic innovations influencing subsequent film-making much as did *The Birth of a Nation* in the silent era.

Thus we see both a tendency toward "dia-chronic" correlations in which a sequence of related breakthroughs in a single area of human endeavor occurs under successive Jupiter–Uranus alignments, and also a tendency toward "synchronic" correla-tions in which a multiplicity of breakthroughs in one area occurs during the period of a single Jupiter–Uranus alignment. A good example is the conjunc-tion of 1914, which brought the simultaneous emer-gence of an extraordinary number of landmark works in twentieth-century literature. During the fourteen months of this conjunction, James Joyce began publishing his work—first with installments of *A Portrait of the Artist as a Young Man* in Ezra Pound's periodical *The Egoist* and then his short stories *The Dubliners*—and also began writing his masterpiece, *Ulysses.* During these same months Franz Kafka wrote *The Trial*, Yeats published his *Respon-sibilities*, Wallace Stevens published his first poems in *Poetry*, Gertrude Stein published her most explicitly "Cubist" volume of poems, *Tender Buttons*, D. H. Lawrence was writing the first of his greatest works, *The Rainbow* (immediately banned in England upon publication under the concurrent Saturn–Pluto conjunction), and, just as the Jupiter–Uranus conjunction was beginning in the final weeks of 1913, Proust published (at his own expense) the first volume of his masterpiece, *A la recherche du temps perdu* (Remembrance of Things Past). Virtually all the pivotal figures in the emergence of twentieth-century literature—Joyce, Pound, Kafka, Yeats, Stevens, Stein, Lawrence, and Proust—underwent that Jupiter–Uranus conjunction at a pivotal moment in their artistic development.

It was also during this conjunction that T. S. Eliot moved to England, the turning point in his career, and began his association with Ezra Pound. Indeed, Jupiter–Uranus alignments regularly seem to coincide with the beginnings of culturally significant personal associations. For example, Goethe and Schiller (1788), Wordsworth and Coleridge (1797), Keats and Shelley (1817), Pushkin and Gogol (1831), Emerson and Thoreau (1837), Marx and Engels (1844), Verlaine and Rimbaud (1871), Freud and Jung (1907), and Einstein and Bohr (1920)—all began their creative associations during Jupiter–Uranus conjunctions or oppositions.

Finally, we also see Jupiter–Uranus alignments in coincidence with historic Promethean events in the area of political revolution, often initiating or bringing to a climax the larger and more sustained mass revolutionary phenomena associated with concurrent Uranus–Pluto alignments. For example, the Jupiter–Uranus conjunction of 1968–69 (forming a triple conjunction with Pluto) coincided with that period of the late sixties when the protest movement was at its height, when student rebellions affected scores of colleges and universities, when a multitude of the most creative rock albums were produced and most of the largest mass rock festivals took place, when the "counterculture"—so named during just these months—reached an exuberant climax. During the period of this conjunction (August 1968 to November 1969) there took place the two events most celebrated as culminating symbolic expressions of the sixties' counterculture in the United States—the dramatic antiwar demonstrations at the Chicago Democratic National Convention and the Woodstock music festival. Here too during these months were significant intellectual milestones such as the births of transpersonal psychology, of archetypal psychology, of the Gaia hypothesis. And also during this Jupiter–Uranus conjunction (within 0°6' of exactitude), another expression of the sixties' Promethean impulse reached its culmination: the epoch-making Apollo 11 space flight, in July 1969, bringing the first landing of astronauts on the Moon.

Similarly, if we again turn our attention to the French Revolution, we find that Jupiter and Uranus were in very close conjunction (2°) on 14 July 1789, on the day of the fall of the Bastille, when an armed mob of Parisians captured the fortified French prison that had become a symbol of royal tyranny. In little more than fifty days during July and August under this conjunction, the *Ancien Régime* in France largely collapsed, and indeed the entire fourteen-month period of the conjunction in 1788–89 coincided closely with the major events that commenced the French Revolution, from the initial calling of the Estates-General to the Declaration of the Rights of Man and of the Citizen. It would thus seem as if the Jupiter–Uranus alignment served as an activating trigger, as it were, for the more massive and sustained revolutionary impulse that coincided with the longer Uranus–Pluto opposition that continued through most of the 1790s.

Moreover, during this same Jupiter–Uranus conjunction, the mutiny on HMS *Bounty* occurred, on 28 April 1789, led by Fletcher Christian against Captain William Bligh on their return voyage from Tahiti. The fact that the most celebrated instance of rebellion in maritime history had taken place at the same time as the beginning of the French Revolution, yet thousands of miles distant from each other with no possible means of communication, is the kind of coincidence that supports Jung's concept that an archetype—in this case, Prometheus— can emerge in a collective and synchronous manner in human affairs without regard to conventional notions of causality. That both of these events also occurred in coincidence with the Jupiter–Uranus conjunction, the same conjunction that coincided with the many major cultural and scientific milestones already noted, strongly suggests that such collective archetypal emergence might well be associated with the movements of the heavens and the succession of major alignments in planetary cycles.

This suggestion is further strengthened when we note that the Jupiter–Uranus conjunction immediately prior to that of the Bastille rebellion and the mutiny on the *Bounty* took place in 1775–76, during the very months that began the American Revolution—beginning with the "shot heard round the world" in April 1775, when British soldiers and American rebels exchanged fire at Lexington, and including other catalyzing events such as Patrick Henry's "Give me liberty or give me death" speech, the meeting of the Second Continental Congress in Philadelphia led by Jefferson and Adams, the formation of the American army by George Washington, the battle at Bunker Hill, the Congress's formal Declaration of Causes of Taking Up Arms, the publication of Thomas Paine's "Common Sense," and Washington's victory over the British at Boston.

Given this sequential correlation of successive Jupiter–Uranus conjunctions with the beginnings of the American and French revolutions, it is striking to find that, as an example of the metaphor incarnate, the Statue of Liberty, the pre-eminent physical monument to the Prometheus archetype (even to the bearing of the fire), was both erected and dedicated in New York Harbor during the Jupiter–Uranus conjunction of 1885–86—with France's gift to the United States commemorating the American and French revolutions of a century earlier, both of which had begun under the same conjunction.[6]

Finally, we may recall that the most recent Jupiter–Uranus alignment was the opposition that took place from the summer of 1989 to the summer of 1990, which coincided with that astonishing period that brought the sudden collapse of Communism in Eastern Europe, the dramatic fall of the Berlin Wall, and the rapid sequence of political revolutions and liberations that took place in East Germany, Czechoslovakia, Hungary, and most of the rest of Eastern Europe. In this case, the Jupiter–Uranus alignment would seem to have been enhanced in its archetypal significance by virtue of its being part of a larger configuration involving the long Uranus–Neptune conjunction (rather than Uranus–Pluto, as in the 1960s or the French Revolution). Considering the difference between the archetypal meanings of Neptune and Pluto, it is indeed striking the extent to which the epochal uprisings and sudden changes of government of

1989–90 took place nonviolently, as in the "Velvet Revolution" led by Vaclav Havel in Prague. We see the role of Uranus–Neptune here as well in the pivotal role of the television media (electronic technology and image) in catalyzing the series of revolutions and also in the degree to which these fundamental political changes were realized through a radical shift of vision, rather than a shift in political power achieved through armed struggle.

Saturn–Uranus Aspects

Uranus in combination with Saturn has an altogether different character than Uranus–Jupiter configurations, since while Jupiter expands and grants success, Saturn contracts and inhibits. Saturn presents a limited universe, defined by hard structure, strictness, necessity, gravity, conservatism, control, authority, tradition, the weight of the past. It is obvious that such an archetype would create considerable tension when confronted with Prometheus. In a sense, the interplay between these two archetypes represents a fundamental source of all dialectical tension and conflict in the universe: between Prometheus as the principle of change and Saturn as the principle of resistance to change, between rebellion and authority, freedom and control, innovation and tradition, revolution and structure.

PROMETHEUS AND ASTROLOGY

Let us look at several individuals who have these planets in hard major aspect (square, opposition, or conjunction) in their natal charts: Leo Tolstoy, Ludwig van Beethoven, Karl Marx, Wilhelm Reich, D. H. Lawrence, and Aleksandr Solzhenitsyn. In them we find a powerful struggle against oppressive structures, both internal and external; a peculiar combination of the Promethean liberty with the Saturnian control, resulting in a reactionary radicalism, a kind of dictatorial freedom: "You *must* be free"; a moody irritability suggesting deep tensions between diametrically opposed tendencies, as if they were at war with their own rebellion; painful inconsistencies in their lives between what they stood for in principle and what they practiced in reality; a stern criticism of the status quo, a dogmatic independence and stubborn dissidence, a fixed and obsessive focus on compelling drastic change. Despite their many differences, a deep similarity in these men remains: they have internalized and contained within their own natures the fundamental battle between the Promethean rebellious energy and the Saturnian structures it opposes. Yet, precisely the strength of structure Saturn bestowed on their Promethean rebellion appears essential to the enduring greatness of these individuals.

It is revealing to observe the case of Uranus in harmonious aspect to Saturn, favoring an easier confluence of these two archetypes of such opposite character. Igor Stravinsky was born with Uranus trine Saturn (as well as square Jupiter), and, notably, in the history of twentieth-century music Stravinsky was not only a wellspring of revolutionary creativity, but also the recognized master and proponent of the Neoclassical movement in modern music. Thus on the one hand, Stravinsky could produce the profoundly revolutionary *Rite of Spring*, and yet on the other could compose such works as *Oedipus Rex* and *The Symphony of Psalms*, with their emphasis on strict classical structure, abstract formal logic, emotional restraint, and clarity and economy of expression. As if he were consciously articulating this paradoxical but harmonious confluence of the Prometheus and Saturn principles in his own birth chart, a confluence that he found critical to his creative process, Stravinsky stated in his famous lectures on the poetics of music at Harvard in 1939:

> My freedom will be so much the greater and more meaningful the more narrowly I limit my field of action and the more I surround myself with obstacles. Whatever diminishes constraints, diminishes strength. The more constraints one imposes, the more one frees oneself of the chains that shackle the spirit.[7]

Transits to and from Uranus are particularly important with regard to psychotherapy, meditation, and other paths of self-unfoldment. Jupiter–Uranus transits seem to coincide consistently with sudden awakenings, the feeling of unexpected good fortune in one's life, the euphoria of liberation (recall the widespread emotions during and immediately after the fall of the Berlin Wall during the Jupiter–Uranus opposition of 1989), the happy discovery of childlike joy in the universe, the moment of rebirth. It is the moment of the quantum leap of consciousness (and how appropriate that the original theory of "quantum leaps" in modern physics was first conceived during the Jupiter–Uranus conjunction of 1900 by Max Planck, who was born during the Jupiter–Uranus conjunction of 1858). Jupiter–Uranus transits often coincide with what the psychologist Abraham Maslow called "peak experiences" (basing his theory on two of his own experiences that had occurred in 1927—when Jupiter and Uranus were again in conjunction). In their most exalted form, Jupiter–Uranus transits may coincide with the experience of ecstatic spiritual liberation: Prometheus Unbound.

By contrast, Saturn–Uranus transits in hard aspect often correspond with times of extreme psychological tensions and breakdowns: the sudden collapse of ego structures, psychotic breaks, dark awakenings—the unexpected "return of the repressed." This configuration often seems to represent a vivid manifestation of Prometheus's imprisonment by the gods, an archetypal enactment of the primal fall from grace. Saturn–Uranus can signify Prometheus Bound.[8] Rather than the brighter successful quality of Jupiter–Uranus transits, Saturn–Uranus transits often have a sudden constricting or defeating effect. They seem to bring in the hand of Fate; where there has been excess or inflation— Jupiter's failing—the bubble bursts.

Napoleon is an excellent case in point, his life and chart offering clear examples of both archetypal combinations. He was born with a Jupiter–Uranus opposition and was at the height of his power in 1810 when transiting Uranus conjoined his natal Jupiter and opposed natal Uranus (essentially the same transits that Nietzsche had when writing *Thus Spoke Zarathustra* and that Einstein had when his theory of relativity was corroborated and he was acclaimed as the greatest genius who ever lived). At this time Napoleon was not only the emperor of France, but also the most powerful man in Europe, with his empire including Holland, Tuscany, parts of Germany, and the Illyrian Provinces; he was surrounded by a ring of vassal states ruled by his relatives—the kingdoms of Spain, Italy, Westphalia, and Naples; he was married to the daughter of the Austrian emperor; and his newborn son was the King of Rome. At this point, Napoleon considered himself the heir of Charlemagne. Here we recognize the archetype of the revolutionary being given virtually unlimited power by Jupiter's expansive principle, its "golden touch of success." By contrast, when Saturn squared this same Jupiter–Uranus axis, in June 1815, Napoleon met his final defeat at Waterloo. What occurs on the individual biographical level may also be enacted collectively, particularly when the configuration is joined by Pluto. Just as the Jupiter–Uranus combination showed itself with flying colors in the conjunction with Pluto at the culmination of the revolutionary 1960s, a much different expression of archetypal energies occurred when Saturn–Uranus was joined by Pluto in the Great Depression—from the day of the Wall Street Crash on 29 October 1929, "the blackest day in stock market history," when Saturn, Uranus, and Pluto were in exact midpoint arrangement, through the years of 1930–32 when they were in the "Depression T-Square" configuration. This very potent and difficult combination materialized not only in the heavy economic failure and poverty of the time but also in the crash of the twenties' overexpansiveness and illusions, in the rise of Fascist totalitarianism leading to World War II, and in countless examples of traumatic personal hardships. Economists are still unable to account adequately for this sudden collapse which shook the world's structures to their foundations, though the debacle is more understandable when seen against the archetypal back-

drop of such a rare and powerful astrological configuration.

Archetypes simultaneously affect each other
both actively and passively. In the case of the Great
Depression, we see the Uranus–Saturn combination
interacting in two converse ways: the Prometheus
principle suddenly overthrew the old structures ("the
bottom suddenly dropped out"), and yet it also unexpectedly "liberated" the harsh demands of Saturn's
realm into manifestation: grinding poverty, unem-
ployment, oppressive physical labor, "hard times,"
and a general existential darkness. This complex configuration can be understood even more mythically:
on many levels, the entire world enacted the fall and
suffering of Prometheus.

A related form of the Saturn–Uranus combination occurred with the Bolshevik revolution of
November 1917 when the two planets were in opposition—in contradistinction to the beginnings of the
French and American revolutions, which took place
under Jupiter–Uranus conjunctions. This difference
between the archetypal dominants governing these
revolutions is suggested in the distinctive nature of
the Russian revolution and the resulting Soviet
Union. The Saturn–Uranus character of the event
can be understood as a Promethean revolution
deeply and problematically permeated by Saturn—
in this case, by authoritarian control and materialism.

This intricate locking-together of two archetypes with opposing characters unleashed one of the most rigid Saturnian structures known to history—all in the name of revolution. (It will be recalled that Marx himself was born with Saturn and Uranus in hard aspect.) All the glaring contradictions in the Soviet style of government—the erection of implacable barriers to keep the citizens firmly liberated, the massive censorship to ensure the propagation of only truly revolutionary ideas, the totalitarian dictatorship to realize the ultimate freedom of the people—can be understood in the light of this primary Saturn –Uranus opposition. The Russian people, with all its creativity and spiritual energy, was under inflexible domination—a national version of Prometheus Bound.

Yet difficult Uranus aspects and transits can be used in extremely positive and creative ways if the energies are not compulsively denied or projected. A classic example of creative integration is provided by Freud when, in September 1897, the entire theory of psychoanalysis appeared to be in danger of collapse just before it was born. In dealing with his patients' reported memories of childhood seductions which had formed the basis for his theory of the sexual etiology of neurosis, Freud was gradually overwhelmed by the crushing realization that, although some of these reported memories were true, many were clearly fabrications. At this time, Uranus was conjunct Saturn in the sky, and both were transiting in exact opposition to Freud's natal Mercury, a configuration that typically coincides with a period of considerable mental tension and disorientation brought on by confusing new information and the resulting upset of previous belief-structures. As Freud wrote at the time, the "ground of reality had been lost."9

Yet this "stage of complete perplexity" engendered a profound and consequential insight. Although many of the reports of sexual traumata were not based on actual physical events, Freud soon realized that they functioned in the psyche just as if they were true and were thus of prime importance for psychodynamics and psychotherapy. The inner reality was the operative one. Thus psychology made the fundamental leap beyond literalism to interiority. Through this collapse of the theory on which he had publicly staked his reputation (a collapse that would have driven a less gifted scientist to despair), Freud discovered the psychic reality of fantasy, which not only provided a foundation for the development of psychoanalysis but eventually contributed to the Jungian and post-Jungian understanding of the primacy of the archetypes in psychological functioning. Besides the difficult Saturn–Uranus transit of his Mercury occurring at this time, Jupiter was by transit forming a trine to Freud's natal Sun–Uranus conjunction, and Uranus was by transit forming a trine to his natal Jupiter: he felt "a sense more of victory than defeat."

A similar situation, although with different outcome, prevailed in Einstein's historic confrontation with quantum theory at the Solvay congress in 1927. Although he had been an essential contributor to the evolving foundations of quantum mechanics, when the final theoretical synthesis emerged in 1927 in the formulations of the Bohr–Heisenberg group, Einstein refused to believe that the universe could not ultimately be understood in precisely quantifiable terms: "God does not play dice with the universe." This incapacity to join the other physicists in the Promethean leap revealed by quantum mechanics prompted Max Born, a close friend of Einstein's, to say, "Many of us regard this as a tragedy, both for him, as he gropes his way in loneliness, and for us, who miss our leader and standard-bearer."[10]

The inner contradiction between Einstein's revolutionary impulse and this intellectual conservatism has striking astrological correspondences. For while the expansively inventive, sovereignly revolutionary elements of his mind suggest a correspondence to his natal Jupiter–Uranus opposition (which at the times of each of his major theoretical breakthroughs was being transited by either Uranus or Pluto), his long-sustained final conservatism vis-à-vis quantum theory appears to be a reflection of his natal Mercury–Saturn conjunction, exact to 1°. Saturn's effect on the Mercury principle of intellect is suggested not only in Einstein's unwillingness to accept the radical theoretical uncertainty and metaphysical freedom implied by the Bohr–Heisenberg paradigm but also in his dogged and unsuccessful effort over the last several decades of his life to forge a unified field theory.[11]

In addition, the Jupiter–Uranus conjunction in the sky in 1927–28 that was so positively exciting for the Bohr–Heisenberg group (discussed above) occurred exactly in conjunction with Einstein's natal Saturn–Mercury, thus creating an extremely sharp intellectual conflict for him. These transits involving Uranus, Saturn, and Mercury simultaneously in hard aspect represent the same combination of archetypes as were present in Freud's transits in the critical months in 1897 when "the ground of reality had been lost" in the psychoanalytic theory. And, indeed, when Einstein described in his autobiography his experience of the paradigm shift demanded by quantum mechanics, he almost repeated Freud's description word for word: "All my attempts to adapt the theoretical foundation of physics to this [new type of] knowledge failed completely. It was as if the ground had been pulled out from under one, with no firm foundation to be seen anywhere, upon which one could have built."[12]

In the history of depth psychology, an equally profound division arose between the leaders of that movement when, in 1911–12, Freud's psychoanalytic group lost a series of members. The most momentous of these defections was that of Jung, who, because of his brilliance and special relationship with Freud, had been considered Freud's favored successor. It will be recalled that Freud's Sun was exactly conjoined to Jung's Moon, while their Uranus positions were in close square to each other. This Uranus-square-Uranus conflict very much suggests the drama of a Promethean rebellion against the previous Prometheus, of Jung the Son overthrowing Freud the previous Son, now a Father. Jung was born nineteen years after Freud, and thus the classic Uranus-square-Uranus transit of late adolescent rebellion was being played out between two birth charts, the younger Jung's chart transiting, as it were, the older Freud's chart. In this sense the Uranus-square-Uranus "transit" can be seen as referring to the evolution of depth psychology itself, breaking free from the materialistic world view held by Freud into a more fully transpersonal understanding as represented by Jung.

Other astrological correlates of this conflict are revealing. As Freud's Sun was conjunct Jung's Moon with the two Uranus positions square, so too was their breakup fundamentally a result of this conflict between the Sun and Moon principles. Thus the four-planet configuration between the two men's charts reflects not only the conflict of the new Pro-

metheus versus the old but also the entire philosophical shift from a masculine- to a feminine-
oriented psychology. As a final corroboration of this
comparison, it was precisely when Saturn transited
this fundamental four-planet complex in the two
charts that the legendary break between Freud and
Jung occurred, in 1911–12. At that time, transiting
Saturn, representing the force of division, fate, and
the ending of things, exactly conjoined Freud's Uranus and Sun, as well as Jung's Moon, and squared
Jung's Uranus, which coincided with the decisive
manifestation of the latent conflict that had existed
between the two men from the beginning of their
relationship. In a sense the entire psychoanalytic
movement experienced a psychological break, as did
both men, a classic expression of Saturn–Uranus.

The Psychodynamics of Prometheus
and Saturn

The transits of Uranus are notoriously unpredictable; and indeed this is the very nature of Prometheus
the Trickster. For those who resist the Promethean
energy, these transits act as intensely disturbing
disruptions. They "make things crazy." In such cases,
the individuals are psychologically siding with the
other side of the Promethean gestalt: Zeus and the
status quo (this is Zeus in his Saturnian aspect, as

stern ruler and punisher—"I am a jealous God").[13] When the ego is so rigid that it fearfully resists all change, it will act like Zeus and be enraged, even panicked, by this unforeseen trickery of events, this unexpected challenge to his monolithic authority over the flow of life—over his own unconscious. Uranus was called "malefic" for such conservative reasons.

However, it is just as dangerous to become possessed unconsciously by the gestalt's Prometheus side. In terms of archetypal psychopathology, cases of sociopathic rebelliousness, compulsive risk-taking and stealing (kleptomania), pathological political extremism and iconoclasm, and even psychosomatic abdominal pain are consistently related to natal aspects and transits involving Uranus.

A planetary archetype can express itself externally or internally, physically or psychologically. Archetypes cut across all experiential boundaries; they know no arbitrary limits such as those defined by the Cartesian–Newtonian universe. If one is unconscious of an archetypal complex, it can emerge unannounced from within, as in disturbing psychological symptoms that upset the ego's sense of control and equilibrium. But equally likely is the tendency to project the complex's energies outward and thus attract events or persons that fulfill the archetype's character: in the case of a denial of Prometheus, for example, accidents of various kinds, rebellious children who do not turn out the way one wants, spouses seeking greater independence, divorces, firings, upsets of all sorts. In general, one feels constantly prey to unpredictable events which serve to make life unstable, chaotic, and continually challenging in uncomfortable ways.

The physical body can also be the battleground between the Promethean urge and the Saturnian resistance. The unexpected disruption of the status quo can manifest as the sudden need for an operation, a rise in blood pressure, an accidental injury. But the physical symptom or pain can indicate a deeper conflict than the standard medical interpretation would suggest. Prometheus's punishment was to be chained to a rock in the Caucasus mountains where an eagle tore at his liver day after day, year after year. This torment caused never-ending pain, as each night the wound would heal in the cold and darkness, only to be freshly attacked the following day. Sometimes this mythical pain can take a vividly physical form: Freud's cancer of the mouth caused agonizing torment of a truly Promethean intensity and duration, involving thirty-three operations borne with stoical courage. Michelangelo, Thomas More, Plotinus, Marx, Dostoevsky, Kafka, Joyce, and William James, to name a very few, all suffered from excruciating physical symptoms. Each of

Nietzsche's books represented a courageous triumph of will over extreme physical suffering, half-blind eyes, agonizing headaches.

Particularly relevant to the Prometheus archetype are afflictions of the liver, the stomach, and the abdominal region in general. Einstein suffered from chronic abdominal pain. Joyce died of a bleeding stomach ulcer. Two years after Napoleon was exiled to St. Helena, he developed cancer of the stomach, from which he died four years later. Beethoven was afflicted for years with severe liver disorders which eventually caused his death. Jung's most explicitly Promethean work, *Answer to Job*, was written in the spring of 1951 when he was bedridden with a painful liver condition. In each case, the body created the bound, tension-ridden, tormented state of the Promethean mythological crisis.

Darwin provides a particularly clear example of this syndrome, as he incurred a chronic intestinal illness as a direct result of his journey to South America and the Galapagos Islands (where he "stole the fire," the basis for his theory of evolution). From this debilitating illness he suffered helplessly for the rest of his life. Darwin's successive Uranus transits in the 1830s vividly tell the story of his life at that time. He left on his legendary voyage to the Western hemisphere on the HMS *Beagle* in late 1831 under transiting Uranus-square-Uranus, the journey representing a decisive breaking away from the stern rule of his father, who objected to the enterprise as being another interruption in Darwin's less than satisfactory education. During most of the voyage, Darwin had transiting Uranus conjunct his natal Sun, a classic once-in-a-lifetime transit for such a significant Promethean experience. Near the end of this long adventure, in 1835, he appears to have been bitten by the bug *Triatoma infestans*, which infected him with the trypanosome that causes Chagas's disease and which remains in the blood many years after the initial infection. A few months after his return to England, the symptoms began to appear (though they were never recognized as Chagas's disease during his lifetime)—acute intestinal pain, disabling fatigue, nausea—while transiting Uranus squared his natal Saturn–Neptune conjunction, a classic transit for the emergence of such an enfeebling and hard-to-diagnose disease. (These were the same three planets involved in the transit that accompanied the beginning of Beethoven's similarly debilitating and poorly diagnosed deafness, which was accompanied by the profound spiritual crisis recorded in his famous Heiligenstadt Testament of 1802.) Then in 1837–38, transiting Uranus conjoined Darwin's natal Mercury and formed a trine to natal Uranus, and the theory of evolution was born.

We have been considering cases where Saturn is dominant and Prometheus is projected, denied, or otherwise bound. The converse situation, a state equally unbalanced, occurs when the psyche is dominated by Prometheus with no integration of Saturn. Promethean energy then tends to be embodied in compulsive and unintelligent forms: rebellious in ineffective ways, stubbornly eccentric or nonconformist, unreliable and undisciplined, constantly proclaiming new ideas with neither substantial basis nor lasting value, repeatedly incurring punishments from authority figures, and so forth. The Promethean energy expresses itself with no conscious direction or disciplined awareness—and thus with frequently disastrous results. A particularly dangerous example of unconscious Prometheus on the collective level is the uncontrolled and unintegrated development of technology with no awareness of either its archetypal origins (Prometheus) or its ultimate effects ("the wrath of the gods": the impoverishment of life by over-industrialization, suicidal nuclear weaponry and radiation, the global ecological crisis).

Only a conscious integration of *both* the Prometheus and the Saturn archetypes is genuinely liberating. Otherwise, one or the other dominates the psyche, by virtue of its unconsciousness, and thereby represses the psyche's capacity for wider awareness with its concomitant freedom. Prometheus needs a structure for his revolution, and Saturn is that structure. Prometheus needs Saturn's hard-won virtues—discipline, precision, balance, control, authority, the capacity for systematic organization, power of concentration, purposeful self-direction, imperturbable patience, the awareness of death and time. In order to bring to birth his revolution, Prometheus needs Saturn's experience, the accumulated learning of many lifetimes.

Until one experiences Saturn deeply and inwardly, authority will be projected onto authority figures, onto Fate, or onto God (as Saturn). As Nietzsche pointed out, "He who cannot obey himself will be commanded."[14] Without a conscious internal Saturn, one defines oneself according to images imposed by and evoked from external authorities. With the integration of Saturn, one is oneself the origin of one's own definition. Then Saturn as an external inhibiting force is no longer necessary, and a tremendous weight is removed. To integrate Saturn is to free Prometheus.

Conscious integration allows full expression of Prometheus and can engender what is often experienced as a revolution in consciousness, a sense of extraordinary existential liberation, mental and intuitive brilliance, enlightenment: Prometheus Unbound. Prometheus is the channel of the creative impulse within every psyche.[15] In its highest manifestation, it may be regarded as the impulse toward the full realization of the Self, the creation of a complete human being. For Prometheus's fire is ultimately the fire of life itself: the Greeks recognized Prometheus as humanity's creator.

Thus Prometheus begins his task as the Trickster—by the little accident that disrupts the reign of the status quo, by the neurotic symptom that upsets the ego's hold on things, by the bits of information that an orthodox scientific paradigm is uncomfortably unable to account for. And this Knight Errant, this Robin Hood in the eye of the establishment, completes his task as the Awakener, who serves as the initiator into archetypal awareness, the enlightener of his culture, and the vehicle of our liberation.

Conclusion

Although Uranus's meaning is so well-established in astrological circles that its name has come to be synonymous with the character of its actual manifestations rather than with its mythological namesake, I believe that recognition of the archetypal identity of the astrological Uranus with the mythic Prometheus can radically expand and deepen our understanding of this planet's meaning. Knowing the name of something, of course, liberates the knower. As Rudolf Steiner wrote, "Initiation consists in the act of learning to call the things of the world by those names which they bear in the spirit of their divine authors."[16]

Astrology, then, is essentially capable of recognizing the marriage of a physical planet with an archetypal form. Astrology thus bestows two valuable gifts to humanity at this critical point in its evolution. The first is psychological: by perceiving the union of archetype and planet, we are more readily released from being unconscious puppets of archetypal forces. The archetypal is no longer that which is unknown, unconscious, and inscrutably omnipotent; it is now an awakened reality within which the human psyche is a conscious participant. The existence of systematic correspondences between planetary movements and specific psychological conditions and events has implications for archetypal and transpersonal psychology in particular. Depth of psychological understanding, the timing and character of psychological conditions and transformations, precision of archetypal naming, consideration of specific archetypal combinations (often those not normally considered in a mythological, story-based analysis), therapeutic effectiveness—all these can be significantly enhanced by a sound knowledge of astrological variables.

The second gift is perhaps a deeper one, and we could call it spiritual, but just as appropriately philosophical or scientific in the deepest sense: the sustained study of astrology grants human consciousness the experience of vivid intimations of a divine intelligence of scarcely conceivable complexity, power, and beauty. By having one's limited rational framework repeatedly challenged and transcended by powerful synchronicities, one's vision of the universe becomes opened to an intimate encounter with the numinous. The archetypal lives and breathes its meaning into us and into history whether or not we are capable of recognizing its presence; but by becoming aware of this reality in the profound ways permitted by the study of astrology, we are allowed the privilege of consciously participating in the creative process of the cosmos itself.

The act of perceiving astrological archetypes and thus freeing oneself from the bondage of unconsciousness is, on one level, an extraordinary feat of human rebellion against archetypal manipulation. It is, in essence, stealing fire from the gods. On a higher level, of course, that theft itself is archetypally ordained, and that archetype is Prometheus. Astrology is Prometheus's fire.

Natal Uranus Aspects Cited in Text

Arthur Conan Doyle	2°48'	Uranus conjunct Sun
Sigmund Freud	4°16'	Uranus conjunct Sun
Richard Strauss	4°27'	Uranus conjunct Sun
Stanley Kubrick	4°06'†	Uranus trine Sun

Timothy Leary	3°01'	Uranus trine Sun
Richard Alpert	0°30'	Uranus conjunct Sun
William James	0°02'†	Uranus sextile Sun
Lewis Carroll	7°46'	Uranus conjunct Sun
L. Frank Baum	3°38'†	Uranus conjunct Sun
Walt Disney	4°22'	Uranus conjunct Sun
Leo Tolstoy	1°51'††	Uranus opposite Saturn
Ludwig van Beethoven	3°40'††	Uranus square Saturn
Karl Marx	3°43'	Uranus square Saturn
Wilhelm Reich	1°45'††	Uranus conjunct Saturn
D. H. Lawrence	5°37'	Uranus square Saturn
Aleksandr Solzhenitsyn	3°52'††	Uranus opposite Saturn
Igor Stravinsky	6°08'††	Uranus trine Saturn
Max Planck	5°19'††	Uranus conjunct Jupiter
Napoleon Bonaparte	3°30'	Uranus opposite Jupiter
Friedrich Nietzsche	7°31'	Uranus conjunct Jupiter
Albert Einstein	3°48'	Uranus opposite Jupiter
Rudolf Steiner	0°43'	Uranus square Sun

† ± < 1° (date of birth only)

†† ± < 0°15' (date of birth only)

117

AFTERWORD

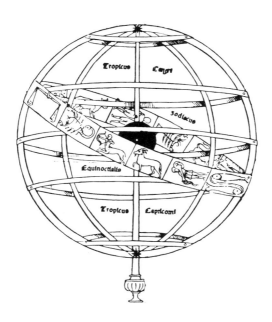

In looking over this essay, most of which was written between ten and fifteen years ago, I notice two important topics not addressed that perhaps should be: (1) the archetypal significance in history of the Uranus–Neptune cycle, the planetary combination most relevant to our own era; and (2) the issue of why the planet Uranus appears to have been misnamed—or, to put the question more broadly, what relationship, if any, exists between the discovery and original naming of Uranus, on the one hand, and the evolution of human consciousness on the other. Before sending this essay off to the publisher, I would like to venture a few words here on each of these issues.

The Uranus–Neptune Cycle

It seems fitting that the various parts and versions of this essay, published over the past decade and a half, have been collated and published as a complete work in 1993–94, just as Uranus and Neptune have reached exact conjunction—the only time in the twentieth century, as it happens, to be graced by that particular astronomical event. For in retrospect, the Uranus–Neptune conjunction seems to pervade the essay, rather like Flaubert's God who is present everywhere and visible nowhere, or almost nowhere. The Uranus–Neptune combination is associated, both in history and in personal biographies, with periods in which the archetypal—the mythic, the spiritual, the transcendent, the imaginal, the numinous—is suddenly awakened and liberated in new ways into human consciousness. We see this all around us now: the tremendous upswelling of interest today in an astonishing multiplicity of spiritual paths and traditions, in esoteric disciplines, in the transpersonal movement, in meditation and mystical religious traditions, in Jungian and archetypal psychology, in mythology and ancient religions, in shamanism and indigenous traditions, in the recovery of Goddess spirituality and feminine dimensions of the divine, in ecofeminist spirituality, in psychedelic self-exploration and new forms of experiential psychotherapy that effect profound changes of consciousness, in the emergence of holistic and participatory paradigms in virtually every field, in the unprecedented convergence of science and spirituality. We see it in the collective awakening of an intense desire to merge with a greater unity—to reconnect with the Earth and all forms of life on it, with the cosmos, with the community of being. We see it in the powerful new awareness of the *anima mundi*, the soul of the world. And we see it in the widespread urge to overcome old separations and dualisms—between human being and nature, between spirit and matter, mind and body, subject and object, intellect and soul, and, perhaps most fundamentally, between masculine and feminine—to discover a deeper unitive consciousness.

Of equal importance in making possible this great shift in world view, we see signs of Uranus–Neptune in the decisive emergence of "postmodernity" itself in our era, bringing the radical dissolution and deconstruction of so many long-established structures and boundaries, roles and hierarchies, so many once-firm certainties and beliefs and limiting assumptions. The cultural consciousness has experienced a shift into a state that is fundamentally between paradigms—unprecedentedly flexible, free-floating, uncertain, disoriented, epistemologically and metaphysically confused, and yet open to possibilities and realities not even permitted within the arena of sensible discourse in an earlier generation. Mainstream modern culture is awakening to the unsettling but ultimately liberating truth that, as a certain dramatist born under a Uranus–Neptune opposition several centuries ago once put it, "There are more things in heaven and earth, Horatio, than are dreamt of in your philosophy."

Given an orb of 10–15°, evidently the usual range within which these great outer-planet conjunctions and oppositions are archetypally operative, the Uranus–Neptune conjunction of our time began around 1985 and will last until just after the turn of the millennium, in 2001 (being within 10° orb between 1988 and 1998). We saw this archetypal combination's Neptunian activation of the Prometheus impulse first emerging in the international political arena with the rise of perestroika and glasnost under Gorbachev in the Soviet Union, and in a widespread intensified urge for international peace combined with the growing dissolution of global barriers through communications technology. And it achieved its most dramatic impact with the great and seemingly miraculous successful revolutions that swept Eastern Europe when Jupiter came into opposition to the Uranus–Neptune conjunction in 1989–90 (a conjunction that also, significantly, involved Saturn—hence the crucial elements of the sudden breakdown of old structures, the end of the Communist dream, the widespread disillusionment and despair that overswept the peoples of Eastern Europe, as well as the presence of practical idealism in the service of radical social-political restructuring).

Thus the first half of the Uranus–Neptune conjunction has coincided with the liberation not only of millions of people from the oppression of the Communist belief system, but of the entire planetary consciousness from the imprisonment of the Cold War and its constant threat of nuclear apocalypse. Also appropriate to Uranus–Neptune, these years witnessed the unexpected spread throughout the world of the Promethean democratic ideal, vividly illustrated in the appearance in Tiananmen Square of the Goddess of Liberty statue constructed by the gentle student rebels of China.

Of course every archetypal combination has its shadow side, and the Uranus–Neptune conjunction is no exception. The collective psyche's highly activated thirst for transcendence, while ultimately spiritual in nature, has brought forth a wide range of less exalted impulses and behaviors. The collective impulse toward escapism and denial, passivity and narcissism, credulity and delusion; the hyperstimulating rapidity of technologically produced images signifying nothing; the hypnotic fascination with and addiction to image ("image is everything"); indeed, the widespread obsession with addictions of all kinds, from drugs and alcohol to consumerism and television—these and many more forms of accelerated and intensified *maya* make less unambiguous the positive virtues of such other Uranus–Neptune phenomena as interactive electronic multimedia and "virtual reality." (We see suggestive signs of a disruptively hyperactivated Neptune on more literal levels as well, with massive floods, tidal waves, disasters at sea, oil spills, industrial accidents involving liquids and gases.) The intensified religious consciousness of the age has given rise to cult movements, fundamentalist fanaticism, and a host of eccentric "new age" infatuations. The dissolving of rigid structures in the psyche permitting the emergence of non-ordinary states of consciousness can lend itself not only to higher levels of consciousness and genuine mystical illumination, but to destructively delusory states as well. Seldom has the need for discernment been more critical.

Yet I believe that a larger historical perspective of the Uranus–Neptune cycle gives much grounds for hope. As we consider the potential archetypal significance of this combination in terms of fundamental paradigm shift, spiritual and psychological awakening, and the accelerated emergence of an archetypal awareness into the cultural psyche, it is useful to recall the extraordinary confluence of events that coincided with the last Uranus–Neptune opposition which extended throughout the first decade and a half of the twentieth century: the revolution in human self-understanding mediated by depth psychology, especially Jung's archetypal psychology and his deepening of Freud's psychoanalytic breakthrough (which continued its own important evolution during these years); the revolutions in physics and cosmology (Einstein's relativity theory, Planck's quantum theory), in painting and the visual arts (Cezanne, Picasso, Matisse, Braque, Kandinsky), literature (Joyce, Proust, Gertrude Stein, Henry James, Kafka, Rilke, Yeats, Eliot, Pound, Stevens), music (Debussy, Stravinsky, Schoenberg), philosophy (William James, Bergson, Husserl), spiritual activism (Gandhi, Tolstoy), esotericism and mysticism (Rudolf Steiner, Aurobindo). The remarkable coalescing of these and many other related events and trends precipitated a radical transformation of vision for the entire culture, as well as the seeds for future profound changes in the cultural psyche.

If we move back to the immediately preceding Uranus–Neptune conjunction, that of 1815–1829, centered around the year 1821, we find a similar emergence of the archetypal, mythic, transcendent, and numinous into the collective psyche with the great age of Romanticism at its height. Here was Shelley, reading Plato at sea and writing *Prometheus Unbound*, seeking to combine the ideal spiritual realm with a revolution in consciousness bringing new freedom to humanity. Here was Keats writing his great odes, beginning with "On First Looking into Chapman's Homer" (where he compares his awakening to the numinous mythic realm to the discovery of Uranus: "Then felt I like a watcher of the skies. . ."). Here also was Keats's influential conception of "Soul-making," described in a letter to his brother in 1819, later to become so central to the archetypal psychology of the late twentieth century. Here were Byron, Schubert, Stendhal, Scott, as well as Coleridge working out a profound Romantic philosophical perspective in his *Biographia Literaria*; Hegel articulating his absolute Idealism in his *Encyclopaedia*; Goethe and Beethoven in their inspired culminating years—the completion of *Faust*, the Ninth Symphony, the *Missa Solemnis*, the late quartets. And here was the great wave of births of individuals whose extraordinary imaginative visions would so enrich world literature in the nineteenth century—Dostoevsky, Tolstoy, Melville, Flaubert, Turgenev, the Brontës, George Eliot, Baudelaire, Whitman.

The emergence of an archetypal consciousness, whether it takes the form of an enhanced awareness of the ideal, a resurgence of Platonism, a new appreciation of the mythic, or a heightened access to the imaginal, seems especially characteristic of Uranus–Neptune alignments, and nowhere is that more evident than in the Uranus–Neptune conjunction of the 1470s and 1480s, at the heart of the Renaissance (a conjunction closely resembling our own with Uranus and Neptune in harmonious sextile to Pluto). Here was that luminous period that saw the Florentine Academy's Neoplatonic revival at its height during the reign of Lorenzo the Magnificent, with Ficino writing the *Theologia Platonica* and publishing the first complete translation of Plato in the West, Pico della Mirandola composing the manifesto of Renaissance Humanism, the *Oration on the Dignity of Man*, Leonardo da Vinci beginning his artistic career with *The Adoration of the Magi*, and Botticelli painting *The Birth of Venus*, the paradigmatic embodiment of the Renaissance's rebirth of archetypal beauty. And here also we find the births of those artists who would fulfill the Renaissance idealist imaginative vision, Raphael and Michelangelo, as well as of Copernicus and Luther, the two men who would initiate the great paradigm revolutions beginning the modern era, the Scientific Revolution and the Reformation.

So also with the major religious awakenings of history. We see the characteristic signs of Uranus–Neptune, for example, in the Great Awakening that swept America during the conjunction of the 1730s and 1740s, or in the great wave of mystical fervor that swept Europe in the first two decades of the fourteenth century (during the conjunction that also brought Dante's *Divine Comedy* and the birth of Petrarch), or in the birth and rapid spread of Islam under the prophet Muhammad during the conjunction of the 620s and 630s.

Moreover, we find that the birth of Christianity

itself took place during the Uranus–Neptune alignment of c. 15–35 A.D., an opposition, encompassing most of the events described in the New Testament, including the period of Jesus of Nazareth's ministry, his crucifixion (during the Saturn–Pluto opposition of 29–30) and the revelatory events immediately following, and the conversion of St. Paul.

Moving back yet farther, we find that Uranus and Neptune were again in conjunction in the last decade of the fifth century B.C. and the first decade of the fourth, which encompassed that historic period in ancient Greece that brought Socrates' most influential teaching as well as his death, in 399 B.C. in Athens—this event initiating the birth of Platonism, and indeed of the entire Western philosophical tradition that is rooted in Socrates and Plato.

Finally, we move back one more cycle to that epoch-making Uranus–Neptune alignment that was joined by Pluto in the only triple conjunction of the outermost planets in historical times, extending from the 580s to the 560s B.C. Here we find the heart of the great "axial age" that brought forth so many of the world's principal religious and spiritual traditions: the age of Gautama Buddha in India, of Lao-Tse in China, of Zoroaster in Persia; the age of the major prophets of ancient Israel, Jeremiah, Ezekiel, and Second Isaiah, when the Hebrew Scriptures began to be compiled; the age when the oracle of

Delphi was at the height of its influence in ancient Greece; the age of the earliest Greek philosophers, Thales, Anaximander, and Pythagoras.

Thus there is reason to believe that our own experience of Uranus and Neptune in conjunction will not be without its enduring blessings.

Prometheus and Uranus in the Evolution of Consciousness

This leaves one other issue not discussed in the essay that still invites our attention, the question as to why the planet Uranus seems to have been misnamed at the time of its discovery.

It seems to me likely that if the planet discovered in 1781 had been known to the ancient Greeks, it would have been named Prometheus, just as they accurately named the visible planets Aphrodite, Hermes, Ares, Zeus, and Kronos. Yet it would also seem that the evolution of human consciousness has been such that Saturn–Kronos was, inevitably, as it were, the outermost planet known to the ancients, circumscribing the ancient geocentric cosmos with its rulership of fate and limit—thus the cosmic determinisms of the Stoics, the Gnostics, and other representative Hellenistic perspectives. It was in fact the Promethean impulse in the human spirit, which fully emerged so decisively in the later, modern

131

development of the Western psyche, that impelled the evolving human self to break free from all cosmic determinisms to forge its own autonomy. Thus the ancient astrology, like the geocentric cosmos, had to be repudiated and eclipsed for the evolution of consciousness to unfold.

The discovery and naming of the planet Uranus would appear to be reflective of that evolutionary process in several distinct ways. First, the discovery coincided with, and implicitly signified, the powerful emergence of the Prometheus archetype in the collective consciousness of the modern era. Second, the discovery directly contributed to the decline of astrology, shattering the ancient seven-planet cosmos and supporting the autonomy-seeking, world-disenchanting trajectory of the modern mind. Third, the planet was named, or misnamed, according to a rationalistic logic perfectly characteristic of that era, the Enlightenment, and of the science that made possible its discovery. Fourth, the misnaming itself expedited the decline of astrology, reinforcing mechanistic science's capacity to construct and maintain a disenchanted world view for the modern psyche. And fifth—and this is the great paradox that informs the whole event—that same planet, it seems, would ultimately emerge as an essential, even pivotal, element in making possible the recovery and re-visioning of astrology, and indeed in mediating the re-enchantment of the cosmos in a new, radically expanded form that preserves and even increases human autonomy.

Why then, in terms of the evolution of consciousness, was the planet not given the name that would have reflected its archetypal meaning? One can only speculate. But Prometheus is, after all, the trickster. And, he is also the awakener. What more appropriate era for his planetary self-revelation than the late twentieth century when astrology itself, which his planet is said to rule, is being reborn.

NOTES

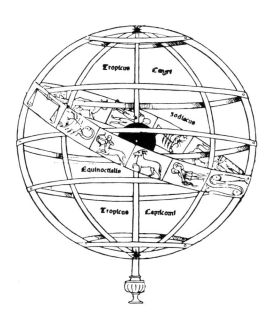

I.

1. For a discussion of the Platonic doctrine of archetypal Ideas and its complex relationship to Greek myth, see Richard Tarnas, *The Passion of the Western Mind: Understanding the Ideas That Have Shaped Our World View* (New York: Harmony, 1991; Ballantine, 1993), 4–32.
2. James Hillman, *Re-Visioning Psychology* (New York: Harper & Row, 1975), 169–70.
3. The distinction between Jungian and Platonic archetypes is now considerably less sharp than it once was. The conventional and still most widely known view of Jungian archetypes was based on Jung's middle-period writings, when his thought was still largely governed by Cartesian–Kantian philosophical assumptions concerning the nature of the human mind and its separation from the external world. In contrast with the Platonic and Neoplatonic view of archetypes as ontologically independent and rooted in the nature of the cosmos, Jung's conception of archetypes at this stage was essentially equivalent to Kant's conception of a priori forms and categories: they were inherited psychological structures or dispositions which preceded and determined the character of human experience, but which did not transcend the human psyche. In his later work, however, and particularly

137

in relation to his study of synchronicities, Jung began to move toward a conception of archetypes as transcendent "psychoid" (i.e., not exclusively psychic) factors that structure and inhere in both psyche and matter, thereby in effect overcoming the modern subject–object dichotomy (see C. G. Jung, "On the Nature of the Psyche," in *Collected Works of C. G. Jung*, vol. 8, trans. R. F. C. Hull, ed. H. Read et al. [Princeton: Princeton University Press, 1968], §§ 343–442, and "Synchronicity: An Acausal Connecting Principle," vol. 8, §§ 816–968. Recent post-Jungian archetypal and transpersonal psychologists have pressed this important development further: see Hillman, *Re-Visioning Psychology* and "*Anima Mundi*: The Return of the Soul to the World," *Spring 1982: An Annual of Archetypal Psychology and Jungian Thought*: 71–93; Barbara Eckman, "Jung, Hegel, and the Subjective Universe," *Spring 1986: An Annual of Archetypal Psychology and Jungian Thought*: 88–99; and Stanislav Grof, *Beyond the Brain: Birth, Death, and Transcendence in Psychotherapy* (Albany, NY: State University of New York Press, 1985), 45–47, 89, 188.

4. The earliest surviving Greek writing that names all the known planets is the pivotal fourth-century B.C. Platonist dialogue the *Epinomis*, which explicitly postulates an a priori association between the planets and specific deities. Written as an appendix to Plato's last work, the *Laws* (and regarded by a number of scholars, such as A. E. Taylor, as having been written by Plato himself), the *Epinomis*, like the *Laws*, emphasizes the divinity of the planets, but then goes on to introduce the specific Greek name for each planet according to the deity with which that planet is understood to be connected—Aphrodite, Hermes, Ares, Zeus, Kronos. See Taylor's translation and

NOTES

R. Klibansky's introduction in Plato's *Philebus and Epinomis* (London: Thomas Nelson, 1956).

5. With characteristic insight, Stephen Arroyo briefly compared the astrological Uranus to the mythological Prometheus in *Astrology, Karma, and Transformation* (Davis, CA: CRCS, 1978), 40. This is, I believe, the first published reference to a correspondence between Uranus and Prometheus. John Addey mentioned to me that Charles E. O. Carter may have noted the correspondence as well, though I was unable to find any reference to this in Carter's published works (personal communication, 1979).

6. I noticed another interesting pattern with this group of women. The Sun in a natal chart is traditionally considered to represent not only the basic expression of the individual will and identity, but also, given the Sun's association with the masculine principle, the role of significant male figures in that person's life. By this logic, women born with major Sun–Uranus aspects would be likely to experience significant relationships with men who were themselves Promethean in some way, a correlation that in these cases seems to have occurred with unusual frequency—thus Marie Curie with Pierre Curie; Margaret Mead with Gregory Bateson; Gertrude Stein with Picasso, Hemingway, and numerous others; Mary Shelley with Percy Bysshe Shelley; Madame de Staël with Byron, Schlegel, and Benjamin Constant; George Sand with Chopin, Mérimée, and Musset; Beatrice Webb with Sidney Webb; Simone de Beauvoir with Jean-Paul Sartre. Cf. the converse pattern noted later in the essay involving men born with major Moon–Uranus aspects.

7. For the masculine/feminine dichotomy in Freud and

Jung, see Hillman, *Re-Visioning Psychology*, 21. Remarkably, Jung's Moon was exactly conjunct (0°30') Freud's Sun, suggestively corresponding to the intimate, virtually familial, yet also archetypally polarized nature of their emotional and philosophical relationship. Many of the fundamental differences between Freud and Jung can also be understood in terms of the relatively greater emphasis on Pluto in Freud's chart and thought (the id, the underworld of the instincts, biological drives, primal libido and aggression) compared with the prominence of Neptune in Jung's (myth, spirituality and mysticism, memories, dreams, reflections).

8. As the Moon is also associated with childhood and the child archetype, I was curious whether any correlation existed between major Moon–Uranus aspects and persons who were child geniuses or unusually precocious in youth—childhood Prometheuses as it were. Mozart naturally came to mind, and I found that he did in fact have these two planets in close major aspect. So too did Orson Welles, who was directing and acting in Shakespearean plays at age eleven and made his masterpiece, *Citizen Kane*, in his early twenties. Similarly, Jackie Coogan and Shirley Temple, the most prominent child film stars in Hollywood history, were both born with Moon and Uranus in major aspect. I also found that the Moon–Uranus configuration, in a remarkable number of cases (Mozart, Welles, Shaw, Greer, as well as such others as Byron and Oscar Wilde), coincided with unusual, exciting, or disrupted childhoods, erratic parenting, rebellion against the family, and with certain rebellious childlike qualities—playful and irreverent impudence, spontaneity, precocity, emotional unpredictability, erratic willfulness—that tended to characterize these figures even

in their adult lives. These same traits were quite characteristic of Jung as well.

9. Rather I should say, no archetype better describes the 1960s other than the one associated with the planet Pluto—but that is another essay.

II.

1. Ernest Jones, *The Life and Work of Sigmund Freud*, 3 vols. (New York: Basic Books, 1953–57).
2. Ibid., 1:252.
3. Ibid., 1:323, 1:354. In a letter to his friend Fliess, Freud once mused on the possibility of a marble tablet being erected one day which would read, "Here, on July 24, 1895, the secret of dreams was revealed to Dr. Sigm. Freud." What perhaps particularly favored that day was not only the transiting Uranus opposition to Freud's natal Uranus and Sun, but also the fact that Jupiter was in trine to Uranus in the sky, transiting in close sextile (1°) to Freud's natal Uranus, so that both Jupiter and Uranus were transiting Freud's natal Uranus–Sun conjunction. In addition, Jupiter was transiting in close trine (1°) to Freud's natal Neptune, thereby creating an unusually appropriate configuration for the discovery of Neptune's *via regia* into the unconscious—dreams. In Aeschylus's *Prometheus Bound*, Prometheus taught humankind how to interpret dreams.
4. Sigmund Freud, *The Interpretation of Dreams*, Preface to Third English Edition, in *The Basic Writings of Sigmund Freud*, trans. A. A. Brill (New York: Modern Library, 1938), 181.
5. Jones, *The Life and Work of Sigmund Freud*, 1:242.

6. Ibid., 1:255.
7. Ibid., 1:351.
8. D. T. Whiteside, quoted in *Dictionary of Scientific Biography*, ed. C. C. Gillispie (New York: Charles Scribner's Sons, 1970), 10:48.
9. Ibid., 10:50.
10. These milestones in the later life of Kant, Locke, Cervantes, Dostoevsky, and Bacon which coincided with the second trine point of the Uranus cycle should also be viewed in terms of their second Saturn return transit.
11. "The years when I was pursuing my inner images were the most important in my life—in them everything essential was decided. It all began then; the later details are only supplements and clarifications of the material that burst forth from the unconscious, and at first swamped me. It was the *prima materia* for a lifetime's work" (C. G. Jung, *Memories, Dreams, Reflections*, recorded and ed. Aniela Jaffé, trans. R. and C. Winston, rev. ed. [New York: Vintage, 1965], 199).
12. Gret Baumann-Jung, "Some Reflections on the Horoscope of C. G. Jung," trans. F. J. Hopman, *Spring 1975: An Annual of Archetypal Psychology and Jungian Thought*: 55.

IV.

1. The case of Sherlock Holmes and Sir Arthur Conan Doyle suggests how an artistic or literary creation may sometimes reflect certain dimensions of the creator's natal chart more clearly than does that individual's own conscious personality and identity. Holmes's adventures appear so effortlessly gripping that it is easy to underestimate the imaginative power that Doyle brought to

bear in creating a character of such sharply drawn lines, one who seems as fully real as perhaps any personality in English literature. As T. S. Eliot once wrote, "Every writer owes something to Holmes. And every critic of The Novel who has a theory about the reality of characters in fiction, would do well to consider Holmes. . . . I am not sure that Sir Arthur Conan Doyle is not one of the great dramatic writers of his age." Eliot adds, "Another, and perhaps the greatest of the Sherlock Holmes mysteries is this: that when we talk of him we invariably fall into the fancy of his existence. Collins, after all, is more real to his readers than Cuff; Poe is more real than Dupin; but Sir Arthur Conan Doyle, the eminent spiritualist, the author of a number of exciting stories which we read years ago and have forgotten, what has he to do with Holmes?" (*The Criterion*, 1929).

2. Basil Rathbone—Sherlock Holmes's cinematic incarnation—also was born with a Mercury–Pluto conjunction, which seems to represent a kind of archetypal Detective's aspect. Cf. the Mercury–Pluto conjunction of Dashiell Hammett, the founder of the "hard-boiled" school of American detective fiction, creator of the paradigmatic detectives Sam Spade (*The Maltese Falcon*) and Nick Charles (*The Thin Man*); or the Mercury–Pluto conjunction of Bill Clinton, who was reported to read on average three mystery novels a week during his presidential campaign.

3. One thinks of Galileo, for example, who also had this combination (Sun square Uranus 1°46', Mercury conjunct Pluto 1°02'). The converse case of Sun–Pluto and Mercury–Uranus, seen in Nietzsche (both in opposition, 0°49' and 0°36'), presents a different inflection of the same archetypal principles, with the Promethean intellect and

communication at the service of an individual will to power and transformation. Darwin had Mercury trine Uranus (0°03') and Mercury conjunct Pluto (3°54', both aspects ± < 1°): the detective of evolution, with an intellectual focus on biology, immensely long-term transformations, instinctual impulses, and the elemental forces of life and death in nature. Jean-Paul Sartre had all four planets in conjunction and opposition. Descartes was born with all four planets in broad conjunction—Sun, Uranus, Pluto, Mercury—and Jupiter as well.

4. The Plutonic element in these powerful works is also apparent, which correlates closely with the fact that Nietzsche's pre-eminent natal aspect was an almost exact Sun–Pluto opposition (0°49'); that Strauss, born with a close Jupiter–Pluto opposition, composed *Zarathustra* precisely when Uranus transited this configuration (conjoining Jupiter, opposing Pluto); and that Kubrick's film, *2001*, was produced and released in the late 1960s in coincidence with the Uranus–Pluto conjunction of that decade.

5. It is amusing to note that all three creators of the classic "psychedelic" fairy tales had Sun conjunct Uranus: Lewis Carroll, author of *Alice in Wonderland*, L. Frank Baum, author of *The Wizard of Oz*, and Walt Disney, creator of *Fantasia*. The heroine or hero in each of these tales— Alice, Dorothy, and Mickey Mouse (in *Fantasia*'s "The Sorcerer's Apprentice")—experiences a journey triggered by magical means into an archetypal realm. A marvelous and inexplicable shift of awareness gives birth to another universe, full of miraculous events, radical changes of perception, mythical battles between good and evil forces, and great dangers. A breakdown of the conventional reality-structure produces a sudden electrification of

consciousness, an unexpected liberation of the mythic unconscious into awareness.

6. There is also visible a striking sequential continuity in the manifestations of the Prometheus impulse in the area of philosophy and intellectual history. We see this, for example, if we examine the major intellectual precursors of the American and French revolutions during the eighteenth-century Enlightenment. The French *philosophes* Voltaire, Montesquieu, and Rousseau each wrote particular works notable both for their marked Promethean character and for their long-term impact on political thought and history. These works were the *Philosophical Letters* by Voltaire, *The Spirit of Laws* by Montesquieu, and *The Social Contract* and *Emile* both by Rousseau. Remarkably, all four of these books were published exactly during consecutive Jupiter–Uranus conjunctions at fourteen-year intervals: the *Philosophical Letters* in 1734, *The Spirit of Laws* in 1748, and *The Social Contract* and *Emile* both in 1762. These were the three successive Jupiter–Uranus conjunctions of the mid-eighteenth century; the following two conjunctions coincided with the American and French revolutions respectively.

If we look across the Channel to the major figures of the English Enlightenment who had been contemporary with the French *philosophes*—in this case, Pope, Hume, Gibbon, and Adam Smith—we find the identical pattern. Alexander Pope's *Essay on Man* (reprinted over sixty times in France prior to 1789) was published during the conjunction of 1734, the same year as Voltaire's *Philosophical Letters*. David Hume's principal philosophical work, *Enquiry Concerning Human Understanding*, was published during the conjunction of 1748, the same year as Montesquieu's *Spirit of Laws*. And both Edward Gibbon's

NOTES

History of the Decline and Fall of the Roman Empire and Adam
Smith's *Wealth of Nations* were published during the conjunction of 1775–76, coincident with the beginning of
the American Revolution.

7. Igor Stravinsky, *Poetics of Music* (Cambridge: Harvard
University Press, 1977), 65.

8. In this respect it is revealing to examine the empirical
description of the Saturn–Uranus combination by Rein-
hold Ebertin, the pre-eminent German astrologer of this
century, in his volume *The Combination of Stellar Influences*
(Wurrtenberg: Ebertin–Verlag, 1972), 184. When reading
these phrases, one should recall that they are exclusively
the result of empirical observations and are not due to
any theoretical conclusions based on an assumed meaning of "Prometheus Bound," an archetypal identification
that probably never occurred to Ebertin. Yet the image
of Prometheus Bound expresses itself quite articulately
in every line, even down to the biological specifics of the
eagle tearing at the liver:

> *Principle*: Irritability and inhibition, tension. *Psycho-*
> *logical Correspondence*: + The ability to cope with
> every situation, the power to pull through and to en-
> dure, perseverance and endurance, indefatigability,
> will-power, determination. – Unusual emotional
> tensions or strains, irritability, emotional conflicts,
> rebellion, the urge for freedom, a provocative con-
> duct, an act of violence. C [Conjunction] A self-willed
> nature, tenaciousness and toughness, obstinacy,
> strong emotional tensions or stresses. *Biological Cor-*
> *respondence*: Inhibition of rhythm, heart-block. . . . A
> sudden loss of limbs, a chronic illness in this sense;
> operations accompanied by the removal of

something. Removal of intestinal parts, spleen, amputation, etc. . . . *Probable Manifestations*: + Growth of strength caused through the overcoming of difficulties, difficult but successful battles in life for the purpose of overcoming a dangerous situation. Operation. – Kicking against tutelage and against the limitation of freedom, the tendency to cause unrest within one's environment, a quarrel, separation, the use of force, interventions in one's destiny, the limitation of freedom.

9. This quotation and following two from Freud cited in Peter Gay, Introduction to Edmund Engelman, *Berggasse 19* (New York: Basic Books, 1976), 53. The episode is discussed in greater detail in Peter Gay, *Freud: A Life for Our Time* (New York: Norton, 1988), 90–96.

10. Cited in *Encyclopaedia Britannica*, 15th ed., 6:512.

11. Individuals born with Mercury–Saturn hard aspects are frequently shaped by a highly conservative education in youth, and Einstein complained that his own was so dogmatically oppressive that after he passed his final examination he found the consideration of any problem distasteful for an entire year. Another remark of his— "My intellectual development was retarded, as a result of which I began to wonder about space and time only when I had grown up" (cited in *Newsweek*, 28 June 1993, 50)—suggests a further correlation with the Mercury–Saturn combination, as well as a way in which even its inhibiting effects may have paradoxically contributed to his scientific breakthroughs.

12. P. A. Schilpp, ed., *Albert Einstein: Philosopher-Scientist* (Evanston, IL: The Library of Living Philosophers, 1949), 45.

13. The Greek mythological Zeus is a complex figure display-

ing at different times at least three distinct astrological archetypes. In his specially favored and golden childhood, in his elevated sovereignty and expansive and generous kingship on Mount Olympus, and in his specific association with philosophy and high culture, he is characteristically Jupiterian; in his moments of punitive and authoritarian rulership, he suggests Saturn; and in his rebellious overthrow of his father Kronos, accomplished in concert with Prometheus, he takes on definite Promethean characteristics.

14. Friedrich Nietzsche, *Thus Spoke Zarathustra*, trans. R.J. Hollingdale (Middlesex, England: Penguin, 1969), 137.

15. In a recent summary of research on the nature of genius, "The Puzzle of Genius: New Insights into Great Minds," *Newsweek* cited several qualities that seemed most characteristic of creative geniuses in the arts and sciences— qualities that suggest why we find the planet Uranus and the archetype of Prometheus so regularly associated with the term "genius": (1) Creative geniuses do not merely solve existing problems, they identify new ones. (2) They form more novel combinations of thought elements and are alert to chance permutations of ideas and images spontaneously combining in novel ways; they possess an ability to make juxtapositions that elude others, to connect the unconnected, to see relationships to which others are blind, to cross frames of reference—an ability linked to an imaginative faculty set in motion by the reconceptualizing power of metaphor. (3) They have an interest in multiple unrelated fields, making novel combinations more likely. In addition, they have (4) a tolerance for ambiguity, a patience with unpredictable avenues of thought; (5) a tendency toward iconoclasm; (6) an impulse for taking risks; and (7) a childlike delight

in what they do. To these are added two qualities suggesting the importance of Saturn. First, creative geniuses work obsessively, producing much that is great as well as much that is not. And second, they combine a certain balance of youth and maturity—an innovative impulse on the one hand, and time and experience on the other. Individuals in whom one or the other polarity is dominant tend not to produce significant revolutions (Sharon Begley, *Newsweek*, 28 June 1993, 46–51).

16. Rudolf Steiner, *Theosophy* (New York: Anthroposophic Press, 1971). Steiner, who often wrote about Prometheus, as well as the essential role of freedom in human spiritual evolution, was born with Uranus in exact square to the Sun.

Other Works Published by Spring

Santeria:
A Pracitical Gride to Afro–Carribean Magic
LUIS MANUEL NUÑEZ

Santeria is a religion like Voodoo, but Hispanic rather than French. With millions of participants in the Americas, its rituals are a major assault on the Western Christian mind.long accustomed to a distant God and toorderly liturgies. This Spring best-seller presents the gods, oracles, spells and ceremonies of a growing underground religion that may make you shake in your bed. (163 pp.)

Spirits of the Night:
The Vaudun Gods of Haiti
SELDEN RODMAN AND CAROLE CLEAVER

A living polytheistic culture and relogion? Yes, Haiti's! Filled with the author's over fifty years knowledge and experience of Haitis, it combines a sense of art, culture and history to reveal the pleasure and piety in a ploytheistic "voodoo." Includes a bibliography, black and white photos and illustrations of Haitian art. (144 pp.)

The Book of Life
MARSILIO FICINO, TRANSLATED BY CHARLES BOER

Attacked as demonic upon its 15th century publication, *The Book of Life* is an approach to images, daemons and planets in relation to health—health not as pills to take, but as a Renaissance way to "have a good day" and night. In this translation by Charles Boer, Ficino provides a guide to food, drink, sleep, mood, sexuality, song, as well as herbal and vegetable conconctions for maintaining balance between soul, body and spirit. (217 pp.)

Spring Publications, Inc. • 299 East Quassett Road
Woodstock, Conncecticut 06281
tel. (860) 974-3428
http://www.neca.com/~spring